Emergency as Security

ALERT
PRESS

Montreal, Quebec, Canada
2013

Emergency as Security
Liberal Empire at Home and Abroad

The New Imperialism, Volume 3

Edited by
Kyle McLoughlin
and
Maximilian C. Forte

ALERT PRESS

Montreal, Quebec, Canada
2013

Library and Archives Canada Cataloguing in Publication

Emergency as security : liberal empire at home and abroad / edited by Kyle McLoughlin and Maximilian C. Forte.

(New imperialism ; volume 3)
Papers based on a seminar held at Concordia University in 2013.

Includes bibliographical references and index.
ISBN 978-0-9868021-3-3 (bound).—ISBN 978-0-9868021-2-6 (pbk.)

1. United States--Foreign relations--2001-. 2. United States—Military policy. 3. National security--United States. 4. Neoliberalism--United States. 5. Imperialism. 6. Militarism. 7. Anthropology. I. McLoughlin, Kyle, 1991-, author, editor of compilation II. Forte, Maximilian C., 1967- author, editor of compilation III. Series: New imperialism (Montréal, Québec) ; v. 3

E895.E44 2014   327.7309'0511   C2014-900050-2

Front cover image: President Barack Obama laughs with former Presidents Jimmy Carter, Bill Clinton, and George W. Bush, prior to the dedication of the George W. Bush Presidential Library and Museum on the campus of Southern Methodist University in Dallas, Texas, April 25, 2013. (Official White House Photo by Pete Souza, public domain.)

Back cover image: A U.S. Secret Service agent stands watch as Marine One descends towards a landing zone near Petra, Jordan, March 23, 2013. (Official White House Photo by Pete Souza, public domain.)

© 2013 Alert Press
1455 de Maisonneuve Blvd., W.,
Montreal, Quebec, Canada, H3G-1M8
www.alertpress.org

Printed in Canada and the USA

CONTENTS

FIGURES

Emergency as Security: The Liberal Empire at Home and Abroad

Kyle McLoughlin
Maximilian C. Forte

"Just as our vision of homeland security has evolved as we have made progress in the War on Terror, we also have learned from the tragedy of Hurricane Katrina....We have applied the lessons of Katrina to this Strategy to make sure that America is safer, stronger, and better prepared. To best protect the American people, homeland security must be a responsibility shared across our entire Nation. As we further develop a national culture of preparedness, our local, Tribal, State, and Federal governments, faith-based and community organizations, and businesses must be partners in securing the Homeland. This *Strategy* also calls on each of you....Many of the threats we face...also demand multinational effort and cooperation. To this end, we have strengthened our homeland security through foreign partnerships, and we are committed to expanding and increasing our layers of defense, which extend well beyond our borders, by seeking further cooperation with our international partners. As we secure the Homeland, however, we cannot simply rely on defensive approaches and well-planned response and recovery measures. We recognize that our efforts also must involve offense at home and abroad". (George W. Bush, preface to Homeland Security Council, 2007).

Fear is critical to the construction of crisis, a component that requires both identification and motivation. The object one fears may be an environment, idea, object, or person(s). The works in this volume represent the collective efforts of the seminar held in 2013 at Concordia University. This introduction is intended to provide a theoretical frame connecting the works in this volume of the New Imperialism to a critical anthropology of security in the neoliberal context. In an effort to contribute to the definition of that frame, and connect the works contained herein, we will offer the following scheme. First, we will briefly outline the neoliberal framework as a social and economic system through which we argue security is a vital component, both practically and conceptually. Neoliberalism respects no borders, and to the extent that neoliberalism is a core material and political practice that underpins the new imperialism, the latter is relevant as much to the U.S. and Canada, as it is to Iraq, Afghanistan, and Venezuela. We thus seek to connect this framework of thinking on security in a neoliberal context to anthropological thought, but that also questions some of the approaches contemporary anthropologists have participated in that sustain imperial adventures abroad. Finally we will highlight some of the connections to be found in the chapters in this volume that may be useful for a critical anthropology of the new imperialism.

The Neoliberal Context

Daniel Goldstein (2010) argues that the post 9/11world has entered a new phase of global history characterized by the "security moment," a state in which interactions at both international and local contexts are fundamentally influenced by concerns over individual and national security. That is to say anxieties over attack, disaster, and physical violence have become essential factors in political regulation, commercial interest, and public interaction. Perhaps no more emblematic of these concerns is the American led "war on terror," about which George W. Bush stated during his address to the special joint session of Congress on September 20, 2001, that,

> "freedom and fear are at war. The advance of human freedom, the great achievement of our time and the great hope of every time, now depends on us. Our nation, this generation, will lift the dark threat of violence from our people and our future. We will rally the world to this cause by our efforts, by our courage. We will not tire, we will not falter and we will not fail". (Bush, 2001)

Waged in the name of domestic and international security, the "war on terror" provides, in part, a contemporary definition of security as a social construct. Security concerns physical bodies, feelings of terror or of threat, and the destruction of property or interruption of commerce. Absent are additional understandings of security concerning stability of food sources as in food security to combat malnutrition or starvation, access to health care, or ensuring that everyone has full employment under the banner of job security (Goldstein, 2010, p. 491). The war on terror and the aftermath of 9/11 cemented a new cultural understanding of security, the foundation of which is built upon a neoliberal capitalist ideology of individualized risk management and privatized response in conjunction with the retreat of societal safety nets and the privatization of the environment. However, Goldstein adds an important dimension to this: security understood in the narrow sense above, "is a characteristic of a neoliberalism that predates the events of 9/11" (2010, p. 487).

While there is always a risk of producing overdetermined accounts that also leave little room for the agency of the so-called powerless, it can be useful to think of neoliberalism as a globalized bundling of diverse concepts and concerns. These have a profound effect on how security is conceived and practiced in the contemporary period. It is a globalized bundle that includes,

> "the dissemination of a universal culture (consumerist), enemy (terror), political system (procedural democracy), mode of hyperconsumption (transnational corporate power, global economy), development aid (substantial U.S. influence over the International Monetary Fund, the World Bank, and the World Trade Organization), and environmental security factors (ozone depletion, global warming), among several others". (Astrada, 2010, p. 5)

The neoliberal context holds security to be that of stability of the market and the guarantee of unobtrusive state structures to economic development (for more on the relationship between neoliberalism and the new imperialism, see Jalbert's chapter in this volume). In effect, this model demands that a country be sufficiently prepared to deal with the turmoil produced by liberalization, in essence privatization and deregulation of the economy and the erosion of any kind of social safety net. States attracted/attractive to transnational capital then become increasingly aggressive in their enforcement of social stability. Too much

trouble from popular movements could mean the flight of investment or additional market instabilities. As Goldstein puts it,

> "'Security' calls on the power of fear to fill the ruptures that
> the crises and contradictions of neoliberalism have engendered
> and so functions as a principal tool of state formation and
> governmentality in the world today, albeit one that is
> constantly challenged and negotiated by a range of local actors
> and state subjects". (Goldstein, 2010, p. 487)

As grassroots demand grows for state intervention for the protection and fulfilment of a more popular will, a fundamental contradiction emerges. The demands of the people represent a spirit
the liberal democratic state is theoretically beholden to, yet at the
same time the structures and individuals that comprise the state
thrive on systems of unequal accumulation perpetuated through
capitalism. When the disparity between the promises of the economic system and the reality grows, social movements or popular
struggles begin to form in response, thus representing inherent in-
security in the continued accumulation of property and wealth
(Harvey, 2005). Such contradictions, when amounting to crisis,
plainly reveal the state's true loyalties to financial or ideological
interests as popular movements can quickly find themselves labelled as threats to national security (as discussed in McLoughlin's
chapter in this volume).

Goldstein, following Sawyer, thus notes what he calls a "key
irony of neoliberalism" which lies,

> "in the contradiction between its rhetoric—which depicts the
> state as a minor player in the open field of free capitalist
> activity—and its reality—in which the state operates as
> manager, actuary, and cop, maintaining this open field for
> transnational business by creating laws, enforcing policy
> reforms, and controlling dissent among citizens whose own
> economic interests run counter to those of industry and whose
> social rights impose unwanted and expensive restrictions on
> transnational industry". (Goldstein, 2010, p. 494)

This understanding of the neoliberal context for security is increasingly relevant as more crises arise exposing the fundamental
contradiction between the declared loyalties of state structures to
their citizens and those states' clear collaboration with transnational capitalist interests to continue to prosper at the expense of
those same citizens, many if not most of whom are already marginalized by the reigning socio-economic system.

As identified by both Jalbert and Noel in this volume, neoliberal securitization "responsibilizes" citizens for their own security, even as state security infrastructures become bloated to hitherto unimaginable proportions. Some thus highlight this process through an analysis of the *National Strategy for Homeland Security* published under President George W. Bush in which "the state assumes for itself a 'supportive' role in administering security" (Goldstein, 2010, p. 492), while "making each of us 'accountable' for and accountants of our own security, calculating the many forms of risk and exposure" (Hay & Andrejevic, 2006, p. 337).

Instead of attending to what some call "human security" (with rights to employment, health care, education—see Goldstein [2010, p. 491]) the neoliberal state, especially as led by the dominating example/model of the U.S., pushes an "absolute security agenda". This absolute security agenda is simply an inflated version of traditionalist concepts of security in the West, as in defence against the threat of external attacks. As Marvin Astrada explains, the absolute security agenda consists of: 1) hypermilitarization; 2) intimidation; 3) coercion; 4) criminalization; 5) panoptic surveillance; 6) plenary security measures; and, 7) unabashed interference in the domestic affairs of select states (Astrada, 2010, p. 3). This compounds the challenges mounted on societies undergoing neoliberal transformation outside of the U.S., in seeing their states increasingly working on behalf of private corporate interests, *plus* serving as instruments of U.S. power: "the U.S. ASA rests on the notion that the international system of states is an extension or an instrument of U.S. power rather than a system and/or society of states comprised of functionally sovereign entities" (Astrada, 2010, p. 3).

In the maintenance of daily needs such as work, housing, and food, the state withdraws. This fundamental lack of basic, "human security" exposes countless communities to the structural violence of poverty and environmental racism. Non-governmental organizations have sought to mitigate some of this disaster by shouldering the various needs that used to be under the purview of national government including vaccinations, food support, and emergency relief. In becoming akin to private, parastatal organizations, NGOs have been presented with multiple crises on which they build themselves further as prostheses of a state-in-absentia. This has caused some to characterize the formation of a new NGO-Industrial Complex where work by charity and aid organizations sometimes resembles profiteering (see Noel, this volume). Lucrative public funds for disaster relief feed the coffers of seemingly countless NGOs which in turn can exacerbate the human suffering of a crisis by providing the illusion of an effective response while in fact doing little to mitigate the suffering of others.

With these circumstances in mind and an all too brief exploration of some of key factors the neoliberal relationship to security we will begin to explore the relationship of these concerns to some aspects of anthropological thought, highlighted by the authors of this volume, in the context outlined above.

Anthropology and Empire

While various efforts that could bring anthropology to a critical understanding of empire have proliferated in recent years, several still group together very diverse cases, including those from the marginalized periphery of the world-system, as if they could all be considered in a horizontal fashion (see for example: Fassin & Pandolfi, 2010; Kapferer, 2004; Kelly et al., 2010; Robben 2010; Stoler, McGranahan & Perdue, 2007; Waterston, 2008, among others). When theories give equal play to unequal actors, we will have great difficulty in elaborating a plausible anthropological theory, let alone critique of empire. The same can be said of mid-range theories that stop short of acknowledging the bigger picture of empire, including calls for an anthropology of militarism or counter-insurgency that focus exclusively on these phenomena (see Forte, this volume).

Instead, there is much to be learned from some of the key actors at the centre of this system, who acknowledge (to say the least) the unipolarity of the new imperialism, which is fundamentally a U.S. imperialism. Thus, for whatever one may think of the speaker on various grounds that however reasonable are not of concern here, Russia's president Vladimir Putin summed up the nature of this American unipolarity:

> "The world is witnessing an almost unconstrained hyper use of force in international relations. One state, the US, has overstepped its national borders in every way....This is very dangerous. Nobody feels secure anymore because nobody can rely upon mechanisms of order such as international law....A unipolar system is nourishing an arms race with the desire of countries to get nuclear weapons...Until we dispense with unilateralism in international affairs, until we exclude the possibility of unfettered imposition of one country's views on

others, we will not have stability". (Putin quoted in Astrada, 2010, p. 49)

Élie Jalbert in his chapter in this volume titled, "Constructing Empire," takes us back to some of the avant-garde roots of neoliberalism and the "new imperialism," the first time they appeared: in nineteenth-century Britain. His is a far-reaching theoretical and historical collage, which ranges from economic transformations, to class relations, to the normative and psychological "adjustment" produced by states of exception, to the practice of torture. This perpetual shaping and reshaping of our normative environment," is the central insight produced by Jalbert's research into empire. He takes particular aim at the responsibilization of the individual under the accretion of liberal and neoclassical ideologies over the past century. In addition, he brings into focus how the practices of empire involve imperialism acting on the "homeland" of empire as much as on any other nation. There are broad and profound consequences of this, as Jalbert explains by noting that, "the rhetoric necessary to justify the subjugation of a people, be it abroad or at home, and be that domination military, economic, or cultural, insidiously becomes the epistemological toolkit that gradually redefines the way reality is apprehended and understood".

In his chapter, "Anthropology against Empire: Demilitarizing the Discipline in North America," Max Forte first discusses the call for an anthropology of militarism, in order to broaden the call to one that focuses on North American militarism within the historical context and analytical framework of imperialism. He also brings the focus back to both militarist and imperialist tendencies within anthropology itself. Forte reviews some of the key, current efforts to re-imperialize anthropology, especially in light of the U.S. "war on terror" and various so-called "humanitarian interventions" in which Canada has actively participated. He invites readers to consider the extent to which anthropologists in academia are positioned as insiders and first-hand witnesses to militarism, and more broadly, imperialism, and he argues that anthropologists, as members of institutions that increasingly serve the powerful under neoliberal regimes, are positioned in a way where critique matters more than ever. An anti-imperialist anthropology serves to challenge the current militarization and corporatization underway in the society as a whole. Moving beyond these observations and arguments, Forte's central aim then becomes one of considering what "anthropology against empire" would look like, one less amenable to cooptation, one that produces the "wrong" messages for power, and chooses the "wrong" focus: respectively, a critique of the powerful and the centres of power themselves.

Unique to this series of volumes, apart from the presentation of more theoretical works than in previous volumes, were the diverse refractions of imperialism considered by the contributors. These include contributions on the gendering of imperialism, as well as environmental or eco-imperialism. Others range from the military-industrial complex, to the nonprofit-industrial complex, to the militarization of media and entertainment, and the militarization of anthropology. The domestication, or re-domestication of the ideologies and technologies of imperialism also concerned more than one author in this collection.

Pas: "The Masculine Empire: A Gendered Analysis of Modern American Imperialism"

Nicole Pas argues that modern American empire-building adopts traditionally heteronormative objectification in affirming its national power. This acts to "project dominant micro-familial ideology that is developed at home, overseas, deployed on the level of the international system of nation-states". Thus she argues that we must understand U.S. imperialism as assuming and constructing "a narrative of heteronormative domestic patriarchy in foreign affairs—serving to empower the home country and its military while simultaneously effeminizing the host country to rationalize its successful heterosexual objectification and subsequent domination". Her analysis takes her through episodes of the "war on terror" specifically in relation to Iraq and particular Afghanistan. Pas ranges from discussion of the history of colonialism's effeminizing of the other (focusing on the British in India), to the sexuality of empire-building, as well as the sense of emasculation brought on by 9/11, the development of "security feminism," the construction of "female engagement teams," the tactical instrumentalization of girls' schools, and finally the unsettling dimensions of the queering of empire and militarism.

Noel: "America's Own Backyard: Hurricane Katrina and the flood of New Orleans"

Through deregulation and the rollback of social services the neoliberal frame creates an environment ripe for catastrophe by making marginalized populations even more vulnerable to effects of natural disaster. This notion is further explored in Angela Noel's work, "America's Own Backyard: Hurricane Katrina and Military Intervention". In New Orleans some of the most vulnerable communities were geographically and socially isolated in the city's poorest wards, epitomized by the Lower Ninth Ward. The historic urban planning in the city ensured that these districts were racialized and impoverished, while wealthier white residents had largely moved to suburban developments around the city. Noel shows that risks already associated with endemic poverty of the area were further compounded by the gutting of environmental protections and the development of crucial wetlands around the city. This destroyed much of the city's natural buffer to annual storms, where the wetland preserves had blunted the flooding and storm surges of hurricanes in the past. Instead, an increasing emphasis was placed on the network of levees built in 1927. As with the wetlands, little attention had been paid to the levee system and the costs of such neglect are to this day only being realized.

The hurricane that hit New Orleans in 2005 was a natural disaster made a catastrophe in part because of the social and economic planning of the last thirty years. The deregulation of the environment and cuts to services and infrastructure such as the levee system were conscious decisions made within an economic framework that prioritizes individual profit and privatization. This privatization of public services extended to disaster relief and reconstruction efforts and was visible with the influx of NGOs and private charities that came to New Orleans.

As Hurricane Katrina progressed, stories emerged and entered the 24-hour media circuit alleging waves of violence, looting, and rape taking place in the city. For many in the media the image of New Orleans was not that of a disaster-stricken area in need of relief, but was instead a crafted and racialized image of a city out of control. Order, not aid, was the first step. Through the moral panic created by media and government, ample justification was fabricated for military intervention in the city. The National Guard put the city under effective martial law, maintaining a curfew as well as issuing orders to shoot looters in an effort to protect property and install the rule of law. Those that were allegedly looting were likely the same people who had been left behind during the city's evacuation because they could not afford to leave or reach the paltry number of public transports fleeing New Orleans. In the city, decades of neoliberal politicking had stripped the city bare and created a perfect storm of deregulation, privatization, and individualization that resulted in the damage and death witnessed in the days before and after the hurricane. At the same time the grounds were fertile for profiteering as overwhelmed federal institutions began to hire private firms to provide the aid and reconstruction that the government had proved unable to organize— these ranged from private aid NGOs, to private military firms such as Blackwater. Resistant to disaster assistance from Cuba, the U.S. opted to have soldiers from the Israel Defense Forces take part in patrolling New Orleans.

McLoughlin: "The Prying Eye and the Iron Fist: State Surveillance and Police Militarization"

Adventure abroad in the name of security has a way of coming home, McLoughlin shows in his chapter, "The Prying Eye and the Iron Fist: State Surveillance and Police Militarization". He argues that the defence of the homeland is undergoing a process of transformative militarization. The strategic visioning of George W. Bush's speech in 2001 can apply equally to the domestic security policy of the American government. Threats to the stability of the state and its economy are not tolerated, to the extent that political assembly and mobilization against American military adventures have become more dangerous as law enforcement adopt a militarized approach towards policing.

Threats to order have become related to terrorist activity evident by law enforcement's campaign, for example, against the Republican National Convention Welcoming Committee, an informal federation of anarchists and other anti-authoritarians who intended to disrupt proceedings at a political convention in St Paul, Minnesota during 2008. The latter forms the case study at the centre of this chapter. The campaign against them involved extensive infiltration and the use of informants, culminating with early morning raids by police tactical teams to pre-empt alleged plans of the RNC-WC and arrest key organizers. The campaign was part of a broader crackdown on protest groups converging on the city in response to the Republican National Convention. Of particular note was the attention that law enforcement agencies paid towards independent media and legal observers which could be considered an effort to sanitize the imagery of civil repression, where only acceptable videos showing police marching in neat ranks or protestors breaking things would be seen by the general public. Like in warfare, there is a clear interest in keeping images of brutality out of sight to better perpetuate the security narrative of us versus them.

In St. Paul, a spectacle of impending attack by violent anarchists was created to justify police militarization and the acquisition of new equipment. A further distinction was made by assuring that the peaceful protesters—or the ones who followed preapproved parade routes cleared in advance with the police—were not the targets of these raids. Rather it was the radical elements, seemingly anyone who did not fit law enforcement's image of an acceptable protester, who were the dangers, not only to the Convention and to private property, but to the permitted protesters as well.

Stasky: "Echoes of Eisenhower: The U.S. and the War for Profit"

Pivotal to the American conception of security is military dominance in all affairs. This dominance comes at a vast price, the U.S. outspending any other nation's military on earth. Yet the relationship between war, security, and U.S. society extends beyond the desire to maintain military bases at home and abroad in the name of national security. Invoking the infamous 1961 speech warning of the risks of the military industrial complex, or the marriage between the defense industry and the structures of the military itself, misplacing power in the hands of an unaccountable few, Stasky's chapter, "Echoes of Eisenhower: The U.S. and the War for Profit," explores the contemporary bonds between private industry and war making.

The economic implications of war to the U.S. are staggering. According to Stasky, including the daily costs of the global war on terror, the U.S. military spends well over $500 billion a year on defense. Actual numbers of employees within the Department of Defense are difficult to ascertain, yet more than three million jobs are dependent on the continuation and expansion of the American war machine. These are workers in factories, labourers on military bases, and truck drivers in addition to the soldiers and combat support personnel. These agents are sometimes directly employed by the Department of Defense, although increasingly the military works through private corporate contractors. Halliburton exemplifies this relationship between profit making and warfare as the company was contracted for millions of dollars to provide reconstruction, transportation, and security personnel. Throughout this process, Stasky contends that there is a redevelopment of the war wage, a concept of integrating the lives of civilian workers into the war effort.

Capozzi: "Spectacular War: Media, Militainment, and the New Imperialism"

The sentiment outlined under the rubric of the war wage above is one that requires continual maintenance by institutions to foster patriotic sentiments. Throughout the War on Terror, media outlets have brought Bush's war between freedom and fear into the living rooms of civilians on "the home front" in North America, where the public is able to experience some of the trials of conflict through means varying from embedded journalists giving a human face to the soldiers fighting for the coalition, to military gunship cameras roaming the battlefield for targets. Philip Capozzi's chapter, "Spectacular War: Media, Militainment, and the New Imperialism," shows the fusions between warfare and entertainment through which militarist interests, such as those outlined above by Stasky, are able to rally domestic support for their efforts and legitimize American-led military intervention as an acceptable recourse for global problems. The "war on terror" is portrayed as sterile: a clean campaign of tactical strikes that are of surgical precision. The war is at the same time a spectacle, embodied by the "shock and awe" campaign of the initial stages of the 2004 invasion of Iraq which saw overwhelming U.S. military firepower complete with jets flying overhead and titanic explosions. Missing though are the images of the dead, displaced, and injured, those on the receiving end of freedom's war on fear, as Cappozi notes that the U.S. learned its lesson in Vietnam from showing the general public uncensored images of war. Images that show the human costs of war make it more difficult for the military to justify their adventures.

These restrictions on imagery extend to the fictionalization of warfare as well. The Pentagon offers material support, such as lending tanks and helicopters, to filmmakers who seek military hardware for war movies. According to Cappozi, renting replica equipment is often more expensive than using real hardware provided by the military, however such contributions come at the expense of allowing military officials editing rights over filmmakers' work. Depictions of U.S. soldiers in poor light, such as attacking civilians or looting bodies, are censored. Instead, the Pentagon desires a heroic image of the saviour soldier which leaves the viewer feeling a sense of patriotic duty and national identity which could encourage recruitment; or at the very least gratitude towards the military for enduring the horrors of war on behalf of the civilian population. Catherine Lutz writes about some of the socio-cultural effects of the militarization of daily life, which includes the militainment and war wages outlined above, on local communities in America, noting that "soldiering expresses a love for the community greater than any other form of work and deserves commemoration at sporting events, school graduations, and multiple national holidays" (2010, p. 55). This commemoration involves acknowledging above all that the military protects the United States from an ever-expanding list of threats which implies that less military would then mean less security and more risk.

Smith: "Defeating Disinformation: Hugo Chávez, the U.S., and Media as a Weapon"

Mid-way through the seminar that produced this volume, the world witnessed the passing of Venezuela's Hugo Chávez. A day before the seminar concluded, another historical giant died, Britain's Margaret Thatcher. Here we faced the deaths—and the popular reactions to the deaths—of two monumental actors in the history of neoliberalism of the past thirty years: Thatcher, virtually hailed as one of the leading authors of neoliberalism by Harvey (2005), and Chávez, who marshaled mass support to undo the devastating legacy of neoliberalism's structural adjustment in Venezuela which, before he rose to power, had seen the massacre in the streets of Caracas of hundreds if not thousands of anti-austerity protesters in 1989. Thatcher who once proclaimed that society did not exist, was countered by Chávez who saw that no society could exist without social justice. What was the popular verdict on neoliberalism as witnessed by the public outpourings following the death of these two? Chávez's coffin was, for days, the centre of a national grieving as millions filed past, and leaders of dozens of states spoke at the UN, OAS, and other international fora in solemn and generous tributes to his legacy. Thatcher's coffin, driven through the streets of London, was instead met by numerous jeers and howls from protesters, some of whom triumphantly held aloft banners exclaiming, "the witch is dead". Songs were celebrating Thatcher's demise were posted on YouTube and a party in Trafalgar Square was organized to rejoice in her passing. The mainstream, corporate media in the global north could do little to contain the massive flood of highly contrasting

images and opinions surrounding the deaths of these two key figures.

Figure I.1: Margaret Thatcher, "The Witch is Dead"

On April 13, 2013, a large "Witch is Dead" party was held in Trafalgar Square,
London, in mockery of Margaret Thatcher who died a few days before. Here the
coffin marked "society" is held aloft, in what appears to be a carnivalesque event
(photograph by Simon Murphy, Flickr commons).

Figure I.2: Remembering Margaret Thatcher

On April 13, 2013, at the "Witch is Dead" party held in Trafalgar Square, London, an epitaph for Margaret Thatcher is held aloft, and reads: "Blood-sucking vampire, war monger. Destroyer of British industry. Architect of casino-capitalism and welfare for bankers. May you rot in hell!" (photograph by Simon Murphy, Flickr commons).

Figure I.3: Millions for Hugo Chávez

On March 7, 2013, by way of contrast, among the millions that came out into the streets in an outpouring of grief at the death of President Hugo Chávez, tens of thousands attended a ceremony at the National Military Academy in his honour (photograph by Eduardo Santillán Trujillo, Presidencia de la República de Ecuador, Flickr commons).

Figure I.4: "Hugo Chávez Lives"

On March 7, 2013, Hugo Chávez's mourners held signs that showed a key theme that would emerge from the funeral events: "Chávez lives" (photograph by Eduardo Santillán Trujillo, Presidencia de la República de Ecuador, Flickr commons).

Following the continued concern with mass media as Capozzi above, Gretchen Smith's "Defeating Disinformation: Hugo Chávez, the U.S., and Media as a Weapon" provides a summary of how U.S. news media, and their privately-owned counterparts in Venezuela, went about trying to dismantle the popular revolutionary government of Hugo Chávez, particularly with the events surrounding the coup in April of 2002. As Smith reminds us, Venezuela was the consistent target of U.S. imperialist intervention from soon after Chávez first came to power in 1998, in the first of a very long line of fair and free, democratic elections.

Unlike any other chapter in this volume, Smith's points the way to some concrete policies and practices that can and have been adopted by social movements and the state to counteract U.S. imperialism, in this case in Venezuela,. This is a valuable complement to the critiques presented in this volume, in offering some glimpse into realities that offer alternatives to neoliberalism, that present a lethal challenge to neoliberalism, and which neoliberal media would prefer that we ignored.

Struck: "Eco-Imperialism"

Hans Jordane Struck's chapter, "Eco-Imperialism," also stands out as an unusual contribution that is much needed, for bringing closer attention the relationships between ecology, environmentalist policies, and imperialism. Of particular interest to Struck, in his investigation of the relationship between society and the environment is, "how an agenda of environmental conservation has been used by the West to pressure developing nations into conforming to international policies which have affected their national development". He thus argues that this has interfered with developing nation-states' sovereignty and self-governance, in order "to maintain the hierarchical order between nation-states, and between the rich elites and poor peasants of all nations," a complex which he refers to as "eco-imperialism".

From this perspective, "environmentality" becomes a new instrument in neoliberal governmentality. Struck does pay attention to the duality of environmentalism, that it can be both a source of continued hegemony, as well as resistance to hegemony. He places his analysis of the role of oil, water, and food production within a context of "unequal environmental exchange". He culminates with the explanation that, "the U.S., through collusion with other developed nations, and with complete disregard for less powerful nations, is enforcing an agenda in which it maintains its supremacy over all others through the control and regulation of natural resources, as well as the flow of dangerous and toxic materials".

Millington: "Potential Limitations of Ethical Critiques of the Human Terrain System"

Once again, the U.S. Army's Human Terrain System (HTS)—the means by which U.S. social scientists (and anthropologists first and foremost) are embedded in counterinsurgency units in Iraq and Afghanistan—dominated many of the concerns of participants in this seminar. Nathaniel Millington in his chapter, "A Discussion of Debates and Potential Limitations of Ethical Critiques of the Human Terrain System," touches on key issues that overlap the chapters of Stasky, McLoughlin, and Forte.

Millington begins by briefly tracing the political conditions that paved the way for the introduction of the HTS as well as the arguments of those for the ethical involvement of anthropologists in military operations. After reviewing the academic reaction to the implementation of HTS. He then turns his attention to the ways in which critiques of HTS on the grounds of professional ethics may be limited. His core argument is that even if HTS' proponents could mount a strong case for the ethical use of anthropological expertise in war, HTS itself is undermined by its own mismanagement and its ultimate failure to reach its goal of reducing lethal violence in counterinsurgency operations.

Even in acknowledging that there is less of the robust condemnation of HTS in Millington's work than we could find in numerous other sources, it is interesting to note how even in its proclaimed failure spaces are left open to the militarization and reimperialization of anthropology. For example, had HTS been successful in reducing the number of deaths caused by war in Afghanistan and Iraq, would this commend the project of U.S. domination? If we can get the "stats" right, will we all be placated and adjusted to the demands of U.S. hegemony? Does the failure of HTS stand in as a substitute for, or a distraction from, the myriad other ways in which U.S. anthropology continues to be militarized and to serve U.S. intelligence? Should we not be discussing the implications of the Pentagon being the single-largest employer of U.S. anthropology graduates? Making more "smart," making war "academic," and making war "humanitarian," are some of the central rhetorical tropes of the new imperialism, and these will surely continue to concern us with our next seminars.

References

Astrada, M. (2010). *American Power after 9/11*. New York, NY: Palgrave Macmillan.

Bush, G. W. (2001). Address to a Joint Session of Congress and the American People, September 20. Washington, DC: The White House, Office of the Press Secretary.
http://georgewbush-whitehouse.archives.gov/news/releases/2001/09/20010920-8.html

Fassin, D., & Pandolfi, M. (Eds.). (2010). *Contemporary States of Emergency: The Politics of Military and Humanitarian Interventions*. Brooklyn, NY: Zone Books.

Goldstein, D. (2010). Toward a Critical Anthropology of Security. *Current Anthropology*, 51(4), 487–517.

Harvey, D. (2005). *The New Imperialism*. New York, NY: Oxford University Press.

Hay, J., & Andrejevic, M. (2006). Introduction: Toward an Analytic of Governmental Experiments in These Times: Homeland Security as the New Social Security. *Cultural Studies*, 20(4–5), 331–348.

Homeland Security Council. (2007). *National Strategy for Homeland Security*. Washington, DC: Homeland Security Council.

Kapferer, B. (Ed.). (2004). *The World Trade Center and Global Crisis: Critical Perspectives*. Oxford, UK: Berghahn Books.

Kelly, J. D.; Jauregui, B.; Mitchell, S. T.; & Walton, J. (Eds.). (2010). *Anthropology and Global Counterinsurgency*. Chicago, IL: University of Chicago Press.

Lutz, C. (2010). Warmaking as the American Way of Life. In H. Gusterson & C. Besteman (Eds.), *The Insecure American: How We Got Here and What We Should Do About It*, (pp. 45–62). Berkeley, CA: University of California Press.

Robben, C. G. M. (Ed.). (2010). *Iraq at a Distance: What Anthropologists Can Teach Us About the War*. Philadelphia, PA: University of Pennsylvania Press.

Stoler, A. L.; McGranahan, C.; & Perdue, P. C. (Eds.). (2007). *Imperial Formations*. Santa Fe, NM: School for Advanced Research Press.

Waterston, A. (Ed.). (2008). *An Anthropology of War: Views from the Frontline*. Oxford, UK: Berghahn Books.

CHAPTER ONE

Constructing Empire

Elie Jalbert

The theme for this research was born of outrage and bewilderment. It came out of listening to an interview with author and long-time war correspondent Chris Hedges (Book TV, 2012), where he discussed his recent book, *Days of Destruction, Days of Revolt*, a collaboration with illustrator Joe Sacco (also a war correspondent). The authors, after having covered war-torn areas around the world, turned to study poverty and destitution in the U.S. What they found was shocking: from abandoned post-industrial towns (Camden, NJ), to effective slave labour in Florida tomato fields, through a Lakota reservation in South Dakota and ecologically devastated mining areas in West Virginia. The outrage was one I was familiar with, the one that comes from a combination of oppression, exploitation, deep injustice, and a sense of powerlessness. The bewilderment came from the apparent contradiction of the First World visiting destitution upon itself. The insight that I thought I had attained was that the New Imperialism was an economic one that had become divorced of its national loyalties and was henceforth plundering the world indiscriminately. The picture, as one would expect, proved to be vastly more complex than that.

Yet, as partial as that initial perspective had been, in that fragment of empire that it contemplated it proved to be naively accurate. There was indeed a strong economic component to imperialistic practices; domination and dispossession were part of the dynamic; but, what came to light was that the relationship of capital to territory, and to the populations contained therein, had never been a simple affair, and that the self-destructive aspects seemed to be embedded in the very nature of the capitalistic process. What also complicated the picture was that behind capital stood individuals who operated from, and were moved by, deeper processes than economic terms could represent—economic domination inevitably leads to economic hegemony, which blurs the distinction between dominated and dominator; it gradually shits the ultimate power to dominate from the physical arrangements that enforces it, to the ideological realm that consolidates it, and gradually to the doxa which redefines the boundaries of perception. The particular doxic illusion is that it is bounded by mirrors, reflecting the observer back to himself and producing the illusion of boundless, open space. The more one's survival depends upon the integrity of this perceptual edifice, the more desperately the illusion is guarded.

The underlying premise of this chapter is that every subtle shift in a society's and an individual's living arrangements creates equally subtle shifts in that society's and individual's epistemology, leading to profound ontological changes—the boundaries of what we know to be true, but most importantly to exist, are in constant flux, adjusting to the ever evolving cognitive negotiation between us and our environment. What has struck me, in the course of thinking about empire, is that decontextualization emerges as a pervasive quality of the modern age, and this can be seen in all of its aspects, be they moral, physical, structural, or intellectual, and has a disturbingly violent potential. What I propose to do, however, is not to provide a genealogy of decontextualization, nor to give an exhaustive account of its incarnations, but rather to explore some of its aspects that appear to be particularly related to the imperial project. The scope of this topic being beyond the ability of this paper to fathom properly, I have attempted to sketch a wider portrait than can be adequately detailed in order to hopefully provide the reader with some insights that a recontextualization, no matter how partial, can provide. By tracing the shadowy, sinewy paths of empire, I discovered a world far more complex than I had imagined which had been the empire of clear, trenchant narratives, decontextualized spaces, and colonized minds. In this paper, I will attempt to converge these sinewy paths into a narrative of my own, but one that hopefully steers clear of reassuring taxonomies.

The New Imperialism

The story of the transition toward the New Imperialism reads like an account of neoliberalism: the rise of financial interests; rising public debt due to defense spending; free trade and decrease of government intervention in the economy' the dependence of the country on economic growth to sustain its hegemony; deep cuts in public spending; and, free trade pushed as a solution that eroded profitability of agriculture and the power of landed interests, among other facets. Surprisingly, this is not an account of the past 40 years, but Cain and Hopkins's (1986) perspective on Britain in the period from 1688 to 1850, leading up to the New Imperialism of the second half of the nineteenth-century. It is worth looking at their account a little more closely as it might help dissipate some of the exceptionalist fog that can so easily taint our perception of ourselves.

The authors argue that "the new economic and political structures which arose—and the imperialism which flowed from them—[after 1850] were not dominated by industrial capitalism" (Cain & Hopkins, 1986, p. 525). Rather, those structures were dominated by the services/international finance sector that had begun its spread after 1815, which put London at the heart of a new informal empire, and carried with it the cultural legacy of Britain's landed aristocracy. A key point the authors make is that capitalism is best understood as a flexible system that adapts to preexisting social and political frameworks (see Cain & Hopkins, 1986, pp. 505 fn. 15, 524), rather than as a static and uncompromising force that acts upon and transforms them. This is not to say that capitalism does not exist as an extrinsic, destructive force—the examples are all around us, but that it is more productive in this context to recognize its adaptive quality, as it informs us of some of the important characteristics that it acquired in seventeenth- to nineteenth-century Britain. In the context of their discussion, Cain and Hopkins trace how the aristocratic values of Britain's landed elite of the late seventeenth-century were transferred to the newly emerging market activities. At the time, a distinction could be made between high status landed rentier wealth, entrepreneurial wealth derived from manufacturing activities, and that derived from the service sector (e.g. banking). Administrators and civil servants "were drawn largely from the ranks of those whose economic ties were with the landed, rentier or service-sector wealth, rather than with industry" (Cain & Hopkins, 1986, p. 506), helping thus to reproduce and transfer the "gentlemanly" landed ethos over to the new capitalist class.

In eighteenth-century London, a financial revolution was occurring with the "foundation of the Bank of England, the creation of the national debt, and the rise of the Stock Exchange", that was the "most important economic development outside agriculture" (Cain & Hopkins, 1986, p. 511), but that was also at the heart of the crisis that was rising during the second half of that century as increased defense spending, a regressive tax system (to politically "retain landed interest"), and the free trade reforms of 1780 were feeding a public debt that was largely being borne by consumers (Cain & Hopkins, 1986, p. 514). The monied interests that were sponsoring national defense with the "production of new forms of wealth based on paper instruments" became the principle challenge to aristocratic dominance, progressively forcing the latter into an alliance with these increasingly powerful merchants and financiers (Cain & Hopkins, 1986, p. 512). The point of highlighting this alliance is that "the industrial revolution [that] emerged out of an already highly successful capitalist system took place without any fundamental transformation of property ownership" (Cain & Hopkins, 1986, p. 509), carrying the aristocratic, legitimating Lockean philosophy of private property into the industrial-financial capitalism that emerged, and contributing to shaping labour relations as we know them. It is interesting to note that the assumption that private property and capital legitimate the ownership of labour and the produced added value has been a long hard-fought ideological battle that capitalists seem to have only recently won since the 1970s (see Ware [1935] for a revealing account of industrial capitalism in the U.S.; see also Noam Chomsky Videos [2011]).

The emerging relationship between the state and the growing financial sector should also be emphasized. The creation of government promissory notes towards the end of the eighteenth-century and introduced the possibility of waging war on credit (Strange, 1999, p. 347), a useful development as Britain was busy warring against revolutionary France (Somers & Block, 2005, p. 266). Perhaps more importantly this cultivated the interdependence between state and market: the former depending "on the financial system that private entrepreneurs had developed to create credit," and the latter relying on state legal institutions to provide the security and confidence necessary for the development and enforcement of contractual relations and property rights (Strange,

1999, p. 348). One important aspect to take away from this relationship is that there was an increasing awareness after 1800 that the ability for "national defense" was now dependent on "the pace of economic growth" (Cain & Hopkins, 1986).

The French revolution and the ensuing French Wars, besides contributing to Britain's deficit, also had, in combination with the ongoing transformation of English society, a more pernicious effect. Britain had a significant pre-industrial welfare system put in place through the Poor Laws of 1597 and 1601 which, "obligated each parish to provide relief to those in need from sickness, old age, absence of parental support, or unemployment, as long as they had legal 'settlement' in the locality" (Somers & Block, 2005, p. 266). As the eighteenth-century drew to a close, most of the working class became increasingly dependent on poor relief to supplement its household budget. The disastrous harvest of 1795, combined with the war and "a spike in the price of wheat" due to limitations on food imports provoked a "wave of food riots" (Somers & Block, 2005, p. 266). The revolutionary threat, made all the more salient by the French revolution, motivated the elite toward policies of appeasement, but this proved only temporary, as high unemployment and a depressed rural economy returned to the foreground of debate after the end of the Napoleonic Wars in 1815 (Somers & Block, 2005, p. 267). As economic growth became less and less dependent on the poor's working capacity and increasingly on finance, the service sector, and foreign goods, sustaining the poor lost its immediate economic logic. As the economic, social, and political landscape was shifting, what occurred was a shift in paradigm and an ensuing ideological onslaught on the very conception of society.

Britain's old Poor Law was rooted in the conception of "the poor" being "everyone other than the 'idle' rich" (Somers & Block, 2005, p. 268). Indeed, the "first foundational precept of mercantilism [was] that 'People are the Wealth of a Nation'," the second being that the more workers there are, the better. It was understood that unemployment and poverty were due to structural forces, and the political will to counterbalance these forces through redistributive policies were rooted in a mercantilist institutional pragmatism that understood reason to be the human tool for prosperity against the disorderliness of nature. Proper social function was achieved through the regulated application of rational political policy (Somers & Block, 2005, p. 269).

However, as social and economic conditions began to change, competing ideas became increasingly popular among the elite. Somers and Block trace the paradigm shift to Malthus' thesis which saw the Poor Laws not as a tool with which to fight poverty, but as generating the very poverty which they sought to alleviate. The crucial point was made by Townsend whose social naturalism applied Locke's state and market dichotomy to his own principles of natural versus unnatural, where civil society and its economic exchanges were understood to be predictable, spontaneous, and subject to the laws of nature, whereas government was seen as coercive, perverse, and arbitrary, corrupting the naturally harmonious and self-preserving dynamics of nature. It is this ideology that still pervades Anglo-American political and economic philosophy, and is championed in a particularly enthusiastic way by market fundamentalists and U.S. libertarians. Malthus, in his obsessive concern with the impending doom brought on by compound population growth, posited that by canceling nature's check on population growth through natural scarcity of resources, social welfare policies were bringing society to the brink of destruction. Scarcity was thought to discipline humans to lower reproduction rates, whereas artificial sustenance created a culture of entitlement promoting "irresponsible sexuality, sloth, and moral degradation" (Somers & Block, 2005, p. 270). With this logic, it was political reason and intervention that should be mistrusted for creating poverty and perversity by constraining nature's disciplining laws.

By obscuring the structural forces behind poverty and presenting them as behavioral ones, Malthus changed the terms of the debate from one of class relations to one of morality, making the poor and the unemployed responsible for their own condition by shifting causality from structural to intrinsic—poverty was now understood as flaw of character, a moral failing that put the blame squarely on the individual and erased notions of preconditioned advantage. His theories gave the elites the "scientific" leverage with which to promote their anti-welfare positions as scientific truth, rooted in the laws of nature, and as such making the transformational process inevitable. Again, this should sound familiar, as it resonates all too well with Thatcher's "there is no alternative" slogan for neoliberal reform. We might also highlight the continuation of the above mentioned paradigm shift by pointing out that this conception of personal moral responsibility has also been expanded to apply to wider social bodies and political institutions as well. Under the aegis of neoliberalism, as ever expanding markets are pushed as a solution for reforming a dysfunctional market fundamentalism, it is the governments of these emerging markets that are blamed for financial crises, rather than the volatile and panic-prone "liberalized short-term capital flows" and the constraints they put on governments attempting to implement constructive development policies (Soederberg, 2001, p. 463).

It is interesting to note that the discontent that was growing among the working class from late eighteenth-century onwards was largely directed at industrialists rather than at the landed aristocrats who, being removed from the production process, retained their image as "natural" leaders before their "more fragmented and less class-conscious workforce" (Cain & Hopkins 1986, p. 508). However, it was mostly the new gentlemanly elite, born of the growing alliance between the old aristocratic guard and the new financial sector, that was initiating a gradual withdrawal of the state from direct intervention in the economy—massive cuts were made in public spending at the end of the Napoleonic Wars in 1815, and tariffs were reduced in the 1820s (Cain & Hopkins 1986, p. 515); competition, falling prices, excess capacity, and low profitability, the depression of 1837-1842, the rise of urban unemployment—all of these factors meant that free trade was pushed hard as a solution. The repeal of the Corn Laws "eroded the profitability of arable agriculture in Britain" and, with it, the wealth and power of the landed interest, further tilting the balance of power toward the urban financial sector. Legislation was passed to enforce free trade between 1840 and 1860.

The underlying shift in power is significant. While the trend during the eighteenth-century had been of commercial oligopoly, landed oligarchy, and government financing through custom and excise duties on overseas trade (leading to a high tariff regime), the transformations discussed above led to free trade policies, government finance through income tax (Cain & Hopkins 1986, pp. 518–519) and a credit system highly dependent on the economic prosperity of an increasingly wealthy and influential finance sector in the City. The formal empire was extended after 1815 by an informal one made possible by the destruction of the French navy, reducing the need for direct political influence and providing some autonomy in the search for new markets which was compatible with a vision of "cheap government" (Cain & Hopkins 1986, p. 522). The commitment to free-markets was accompanied in the 1830s by the determination to "export abroad the same self-regulating system which was transforming British society"—it demonstrated the willingness "to impose free trade on reluctant rulers, to evict recalcitrant ones, and to advance 'legitimate commerce' by putting down African slave trade" (Gavin quoted in Cain & Hopkins 1986, p. 523). Rooted in the fear of social breakdown, and looking for "overseas solutions to domestic problems," interventionist policies abroad were intensified (Cain & Hopkins 1986, p. 523). The failure of these interventionist policies "to extend British economic influence ... increased the pressure to adopt complete free trade in the 1840s" (Cain & Hopkins 1986, p. 524).

The new imperialism that grew out of this period favored informal economic dominance motored by free trade over colonial preferences. The main lesson that seems to emanate from the colonial phase of empire is that direct control is costly and thoroughly unnecessary if one discards the machismo of overt territorial supremacy—unnecessary to the principle objective of economic benefit, best acceded through economic hegemony. The only justification for government use of military force abroad is to enforce compliance upon a recalcitrant world population. The dynamics explored above—the relation of capital to political policy and the constant negotiation between rulers and the parties that control the wealth, the ideological vehicle of elite interest, and the shifting doxa that subtly alters the terms of the debate—will help us untangle some of the exceptionalist, mythologizing rhetoric that clouds understanding of the deeper dynamics of our contemporary empire.

To Colonize or Not to Colonize

Before moving onward to our examination of U.S. imperialism, it is interesting to make a few comments about this new "gentlemanly capitalist" class (Cain & Hopkins 1986, 1987) that emerged out of the alliance between the British landed aristocracy and the budding financial services sector, as it is the first time that a phase identified as the "new imperialism" occurred.

One salient point is that economic development was not coterminous with the industrial revolution, but rather depended on non-industrial activities that were "associated with high status and gave access to political influence" (Cain & Hopkins, 1987, p. 18). Additionally, this new category of capitalist that arose out of the decline of the old political economy after the American Revolution fundamentally shaped the new one that replaced it, spreading its liberal values and ideologies in the process. In this new financial order, wealth was divorced from industrial production, leading to industrial retardation in Britain (as opposed to protectionist imperial Germany (Cain & Hopkins, 1987, p. 7), which further exacerbated the conditions discussed earlier but that ironically further justified the implementation of their new economic ethos. Open markets and the increase in invisible income brought wealth but also high competition, deindustrialization, and urbanization. It also fragmented the empire and eroded its power. The British economy was split between a southern consumer, trade, and finance establishment centered in London, and a northern productive industry, whose growth and trade began to decrease visibly after 1870—counterbalanced by an increase in invisibles through the spread of service capitalism that put London at the nexus of "both domestic and foreign savings" (Cain & Hopkins, 1987, p. 3). Steinmetz (2005, p. 352) points out the relationship between economic hegemony and territorial colonial practice, showing how as hegemony collapses, the need to revert to more physical forms of domination arises (e.g. Britain's annexation of Chinese coastal areas starting in1898). This dynamic is important to keep in mind as it provides insight into the more overt forms of military intervention that the U.S. has reverted to in recent years as neoliberal policies become harder to legitimate. Indeed, it is useful to understand the London's "expanding financial power" of the second half of the nineteenth-century, and particularly after 1870, as offsetting Britain's "dwindling economic influence in the U.S. and Europe" (Cain & Hopkins 1987, p. 11). Britain's increasing dependence on international trade brought her increased vulnerability as well, a vulnerability equally felt by those countries dependent on her foreign investment (e.g. in the 1890s Brazil, Australia, and Argentina underwent "structural adjustments" to regain funds from London) (Cain & Hopkins 1987, pp. 8–11). The growing influence of the U.S. on the world stage, particularly of New York finance after 1914, combined with Britain's "inability to meet rising defense costs" after 1918, increased Britain's vulnerability and forced it to rely more on formal empire than finance and trade (Cain & Hopkins 1987, pp. 14, 16).

The U.S. also engaged in colonial and imperial practices of its own. Beginning in 1898 with the annexation of Hawaii, the invasion of Puerto Rico, and the "liberation" of Cuba and the Philippines from Spain (see Chomsky, 1998, for a discussion of U.S. interventionist policy from 1898 to 1998), a dynamic process started that would transform domestic policies (McCoy & Scarano, 2009). The authors argue that "the sum of these changes in the realm of policing, drug prohibition, public health, and environmental management gave the federal government an unprecedented ability to impose coercive social controls, producing a radical change in the American social contract between the state and the individual" (McCoy & Scarano, 2009, p. 17). It also began a process that would lead the U.S. to global hegemony.

After its initial bout of territorial expansion, the overreached, putative domestic defensive army of the U.S., turned imperial tool of conquest, was caught off guard by WWI, and provoked anti-imperial sentiment that initiated a gradual withdrawal from the Pacific (though with an escalation of intervention in the Caribbean and Central America: Mexico in 1914, Haiti from 1915 to 1934, and the Dominican Republic from 1916 to 1924 (McCoy & Scarano, 2009, p. 18). This general trend gradually shifted the U.S. away from colonial territorial ambitions to imperial development of economic interests (McCoy & Scarano, 2009, p. 19), establishing a new defensive perimeter on the Hawaii-Panama-Caribbean line. The emerging new Pax Americana, particularly between 1944 and 1971 during the Bretton Woods era, brought a new form of disciplining measures to international relations that were embedded in a transnational debt architecture; rather than overtly intervene militarily when a state proved recalcitrant, sanctions and incentives could now be used (Soederberg, 2005). This is where the precursor to the "structural adjustment" we are familiar with emerged. In exchange for IMF development loans, countries had to obey certain conditions and prescriptions (Soederberg, 2005, p. 929). The international credit system introduced the incentive of creditworthiness to domestic rule, spreading access to financial aid but also an insidious form of structural normativeness, molded on a reified model of development. Also insidious, but perhaps more overtly damaging, was that this system of transnational debt was also introducing what Soederberg calls the "Golden Noose", leading to what Harvey (2005) has termed "accumulation by dispossession," resulting in the dramatic rise of inequality worldwide since the 1980s. Before looking at some of the aspects that have led to the rise of the "Washington Consensus" at the end of that decade, I feel it is important to discuss some of the aspects that played a determining role in shaping the American persona.

Empire of Contradictions

U.S. history is fraught with contradiction. There seems to have been a persistent divide between its represented self-image and its actions in the world. It has viewed itself as a land of the free, where individuals have free reign to maximize their wealth and pursue happiness without the constraints of government inhibiting their freedom, while ignoring the way in which government typically enforced the rights of one group over another (McCaull, 1976) and provided the infrastructure and investments that made development possible (Novak, 2008; Limerick, 2012). It has promoted its exceptional nature and asserted its difference from all previous empires, advocating fundamental human rights and opportunity for all, though its society has been one of profound segregation (Perlstein, 2006), with a foreign policy more often than not brutal, repressive, and indeed essentially imperialistic (Chomsky, 1998; McCoy, 2009)—a foreign policy that then in turn transformed domestic policy by importing its policing practices back home (McCoy & Scarano, 2009; Chomsky, 1999; De Genova, 2010; Steinmetz, 2005, pp. 357–361). Founded on the genocide of its Indigenous population, the U.S. has defined its brave and free persona by glorifying its revolution that shook off the empire's grip, yet has been leading a global counterinsurgent "War on Terrorism" that defines resistance as a threat that must be eliminated.

One such contradiction—the contrast of a projected benign history of the quest for freedom and rights with the reality of American ascent to global domination—is discussed by Novak (2008). In addressing what he calls the "myth of the 'weak' American state", he shows how there is "an almost pathological tendency to confuse American ideal with historical political reality," and a constant tension between "liberty and power, freedom and authority, contract and coercion, and law and violence" (Novak, 2008, p. 754). In the author's view, the myth of an American weak state has its roots in an exceptionalist view of the U.S as being a new world exempted from previous political histories by a "so-called 'natural' development of individualism, private rights, civil society, free labour, and a free economy" (Novak, 2008, pp. 754–755). McCaull (1976) considers this sense of exceptionalism to be underpinned by a Spencerian theory of social evolution that presents American industry as the pinnacle of man's ever ascending rise to perfection. This "social Darwinism" that applied biological notions of survival of the fittest to human society provided legitimacy for rapacious and competitive social and economic practices by presenting them as a natural and normal continuation of evolution toward complexity. Spencer's theory was thus co-opted by American industrialists as a powerful "scientific" tool of laissez faire capitalism legitimation, reminiscent of the Malthusian arguments discussed earlier, that rooted their reasoning in the laws of nature so as to give them an air of inevitability.

The irony was that while the laissez faire capitalists were advocating for government non-intervention, they were using the courts to counter the labour movement. McCaull finds the legal watershed moments to be the 1873 dissents in the Slaughter-House Cases that paved the way for the 1886 Supreme Court decision giving corporations Fourteenth Amendment protection as flesh-and-blood individuals to their economic activities, treating these activities as material property fundamental to their constitutional freedom. Liberty was conceived of as non-interference in the rights of corporations and workers to contract as they pleased. However, it turned out that corporate rights had considerably more weight than workers' rights, and when conflicts arose, such as during the Chicago Pullman strike of 1894, "the courts stepped in to issue antipicketing injunctions favorable to the corporations" (McCaull, 1976, p. 27). The underlying logic was that corporation were naturally beneficial to society "since they were more efficient in both accumulation and use of capital"—both vehicles of the onward march to social perfection. What was disregarded by the courts was that the very corporate growth that was being protected against labour organization was also eroding competition (McCaull, 1976, p. 26). This judicial enforcement of laissez faire was only overturned in 1937 when the court recognized that unequal bargaining power could lead to worker exploitation and, following that, the notion that the Constitution should protect absolute economic freedom was systematically shot down. These developments ushered in an era of Keynesian state intervention through stimulus, social programs, and Fordist compact between labour and capitalists that lasted until the late 60s when global capitalism came into a state of crisis that shifted the structural agreements back toward non-interventionist free market policies, first experimented with in Pinochet's Chile by the "Chicago Boys," and then imported back into Thatcher's Britain and Reagan's America. What evolved from there was what we now know as neoliberal policy, that fundamentally reversed the trend of rising labour power in favor of the capitalist class (Harvey, 2005) and sent the world spiraling into a series of debt crises provoked by volatile, speculative foreign investments in a deregulated financial environment, privatization of state and public assets, and the gearing of domestic economies toward export, among many other interrelated factors (Soederberg, 2001, 2005; Harvey, 2005; Foster & McChesney, 2012).

Personal income trends in the U.S. also reveal a pattern of dramatic reversals. Babones (2012) reveals that the median male income rose steadily between the 1860s and 1960s, and then dramatically between 1965 and 1973. Since then, however, it has fallen by 7.4%, even as the U.S. economy doubled. If one looks at the income distribution per age group the picture is even grimmer, as it comes to light that the younger the age group the sharper the decline in income, with 25 to 34 year old men seeing their income drop by 26.7%. While the introduction of women into the workforce and an aging population have had a role to play in these figures, the main culprit is rising inequality, as 58% of income growth in the U.S. between 1976 and 2007 has gone to the top 1%. In other words, for the period between 1870 and 1970 the middle class got steadily richer, a trend that was dramatically reversed after that.

Neoliberalism

The vast structural changes in the world economy have played a decisive role in restoring power to the capitalist class: the accelerating rate of technological change, allowing for inexpensive international transport and a globalized communication system that combines speed and efficiency, what Harvey (2005, p. 97) has called "technological liberation over distance," a characteristic of the new New Imperialism. Combined with the political will to liberalize the financial sector, to pry open new markets, and enforce corporate rule through privatization, this has contributed to internationalizing manufacturing and globalizing markets (Strange, 1992). This has had an impact both on state leverage vis-à-vis multinational firms and on labour bargaining power, not only by shifting production locality but also by allowing for, through the deregulation of local banking and anti-trust laws, mergers and takeovers that have deterritorialized power and opened the configuration of the flow of investment (Harvey, 2005, p. 97). This has also unleashed the monopolistic logic of capitalism through multi-industry conglomerates that consolidate vertically by covering the whole chain of production from primary source to manufacturing,

packaging, and sale, and also integrating parallel horizontal processes (e.g. control of legislatures, research and education, the peni-
tential establishment, and ultimately policing) (Foster &
McChesney, 2012).The new imperialism, in that vein, is characterized by monopoly-finance capital and the "emergence of a massive
global reserve army of labour" (Foster & McChesney, 2012, p. 130)
which has allowed for exploitation of labour around the world and
cheap consumer goods in the global north. Perhaps ironically (for
those who still hold the arguably naive opinion that a country's
"capitalist class" is moved by a sense of loyalty to that country's
population, rather than to its own "tribe"), we have also witnessed
the systematic undermining of the global north's labour force,
which is today in a particularly vulnerable position (Pollin, 2007).
Not only are today's remaining 14.3 million manufacturing jobs in
the U.S. open to potential outsourcing, but in the context of national economies becoming increasingly integrated so are between
18 to 42 million of impersonal service jobs, such as "back-of-office
accountants, lawyers, engineers, and laboratory technicians, as
well as their support staff, in addition to the telephone operators
that have already become widespread—thus up to a third of jobs in
the U.S. (Pollin, 2007, p. 124). The main point at the present
though is not the eventual outsourcing, but the leverage that is
taken away from the American worker. This threat can be put in
context of wage relative to productivity between 1973 and 2005,
where average nonsupervisory workers' wage have fallen by 8%,
though their productivity has risen by 85% (Pollin, 2007, p. 123).

The disempowerment has also been felt by certain parts of government. Strange (1992) makes the argument that these structural changes have deeply affected politics, where states now have
to compete with each other to attract firms and, for the case of developing countries, to benefit from industrialization. These global
economic policies are now crucial factors in determining policies
and are shaping the perception of poor countries' policy makers as
to what opportunities are available. One of the impacts is the shift
from import-substitution and protection strategies to export-based
liberalized and privatized economies. Global pressures to stay
ahead of the game, combined with the internal demands of a rising
middle class which has become, thanks to the information revolution, all too aware of the widening gap in the standard of living between rich and poor countries, are defining global competitive
global relations. While states have their territory as bargaining
tool, transnational firms leverage the command of technology, ac-

cess to capital and to major global markets, all essential to states for adding value to labour and material. Under this arrangement wealth is now the source of power that leverages military force, and governments have to play a difficult balancing act between maintaining sufficient popular support to remain in power and obeying the imperatives of capital.

As we have already seen, structural changes in the social and economic structure during Britain's New Imperialism redefined normative expectations. The concentrational tendencies of finance capital, which tended to have more coherent and consensual objectives in policy-making than manufacturing interests, have culminated today in a vast empire of finance that seems to imbue society as a whole with its individualistic, disconnective logic. In the British case, with the expansion of London finance with its wealth primarily rooted in free trade and international investments and divorced from local industry, it did not share the industry's concern over foreign competition, and so accordingly was never particularly rooted in any real sense of nationalism—nor did it have a natural inclination to be concerned with the fate of local populations, leading it naturally away from redistributive philosophy and policy. Furthermore, "it was assumed that matters of high finance could safely be left to the small circle of institutions which were thought to have an intuitive understanding of 'national interests'" (Cain & Hopkins, 1987, p. 6). Given the scandals that have surfaced in the past twenty years over such things as corporate fraud (e.g. Enron), collusion and manipulation of international financial indices (e.g. Libor in 2012, and ISDAfix more recently (Taibbi, 2013), not too mention the crisis of 2008 and the ensuing bailouts, or the deliberate and systematic exclusionary mystification of financial instruments, we can better understand how misguided a logic it has been to give discretionary power over the management of the world's economy to a handful of institutions that are also interested actors within that economy.

Cognitive Ramifications of Structure

A point that emerges out of the above discussion is that power, privilege, and influence are accumulative forces, and that empire can be understood as an entity born of these forces, that co-opts fundamental social processes and puts them to the service of its own preservation and perpetuation. It is a force that alienates and subordinates dominators and dominated alike to its emergent logic and demands. It is built by accretion. Every transformation that occurs, no matter how temporary the initial imperative, tends to remain and become the new baseline for further transformation. This is called the "displacement effect" by Peacock and Wiseman in the context of increased revenues and expenditures during wartime (Tilly, 1982, pp. 14–15), and "the carry on imperative" where those who benefit by actively maintaining the status quo are psychologically reluctant to admit error (Lutz, 2011). This accretion is true politically, economically, but more importantly to the following argument, ideologically. The environment that is shaped by transformational processes such as crises (real or fabricated— what Naomi Klein calls the "shock doctrine") rapidly acquires a normative hue. Indeed, research into the processes of individual and collective memory has shown that "far from being a verbatim record of the past, memory is well understood as a reconstructive process replete with distortions, and at time, gross inaccuracies" (Brown, Kouri, & Hirst, 2012), where individual memories and perceptions can be shaped by what is reiterated and what remains silent in the environment, allowing for whomever dominates public discourse to have a deep influence on collective identity formation. Social contagion demonstrates that social interactions can effectively implant false memories of events that a person has never actually experienced (Brown et al., 2012). Conversation can converge individually distinct memories into a more uniform collective memory, highlighting the true dangers of closed ideological public discourse and the demonizing of dissenting voices: through a form of intellectual inbreeding, discourse gets progressively more and more uniform and less diverse, to the point of becoming entirely sterile and divorced from any kind of reality shared outside the group. This research reveals "a social world that consists of an aggregate of auto-biographical memories" (Brown et al., 2012). This research also provides an insight into how opposite groups can evolve such diametrically opposed and irreconcilable views, where even basic facts do not appear to be shared. It also provides a pregnant understanding of how the neoliberal elite have become brokers of myth, as the reality they understand to exist is in fact a repeatedly tailored, crafted representation, a weeding of sorts, that ever attempts to condense plural reality into a static, two-dimensional plane. Their frame of reference is this collective construction, rather than the ongoing process of life. It provides a more productive way of understanding how they can systematically push evidence and counter-discourse aside and justify their claims with blatant falsifications.

The striking contradiction between evidence and rhetoric that is endemic to U.S. imperialistic practice has come to the fore since the 9/11 attacks and the ensuing "War on Terrorism," and has had dramatic consequences not just for populations across the world, but for American citizens as well. It will be of some use to provide some historical context in order to shed some light on the violence we are currently witnessing.

The Cannibalistic Empire

Government documentation that was released in 1973 revealed "a systematic and extensive program of terror, disruption, intimidation, and instigation of violence" directed against left-leaning and activist elements within the U.S. (Chomsky, 1999, pp. 304–305). The U.S. Senate's (1976) "Final Report of the Select Committee to Study Governmental Operations with Respect to Intelligence Activities" found that between 1936, when domestic intelligence was reestablished, and 1976, there had been a "relentless expansion of domestic intelligence activity beyond investigation of criminal conduct toward the collection of political intelligence and the launching of secret offensive actions against Americans," particularly targeting groups advocating against war and for the improvement of "the conditions of racial minorities". Domestic espionage was first ordered by presidential decree between 1936 and 1945; between 1946 and 1963 such domestic programs became a permanent government feature with virtual independence, greater scope, effecting disruption and neutralization of subversives, and illegal and intrusive surveillance; and, between 1964 and 1976, with a broadened range of targets outside of Cold War communist threats, domestic intelligence was broadened further to include activists in general (U.S. Senate, 1976). Chomsky (1999) discusses the various techniques used under COINTELPRO (Counter Intelligence Program) and the FBI in the 1960s, such as utilization of media contacts for propaganda, incitation and provocation of gang violence (e.g. to counteract the city of San Diego's attempt at promoting peace among the black community), and financing and arming of right-wing terrorist groups to perform acts of terrorism against the left. Part of those repressive roots can be traced back to the post-World War I "Red Scare" that saw a wave of repressive activities against the labour movement, perceived as menacing established privileges. Indeed, the 1919 steel strike was labeled a "red conspiracy" and a "grave moral wrong" by president Wilson, "red-soaked in the doctrines of Bolshevism" (Chomsky, 1999, p. 321). This dichotomizing and demonizing ideology, along with its rhetoric of having to defend freedom from the "red: onslaught, also served to legitimate foreign interventionist policy after WWII. Chomsky quotes the Attorney General of the time, Alexander Palmer, as seeing "no distinction between 'theoretical ideas of radicals and their violation of our national laws'" (Chomsky, 1999, p. 322). The Senate's 1976 report characterizes the activities of the Justice Department's Bureau of investigation, precursor to the FBI, as brutal and tyrannical. But Chomsky traces the pattern further back into the nineteenth-century, into the judicial murders of four anarchists after Chicago's Haymarket Square bombing where vague "seditious utterances" had sufficed for the police to "attribute 'moral responsibility' for the bombing and to justify their prosecution and hanging" (Chomsky, 1999, p. 320).

McCoy (2009, p. 10) shows how important the occupation of the Philippines from 1898 to 1935 was in transforming "the character of the American state, leaving a lasting imprint on its security apparatus and imbuing it with underlying attributes that can recur in any subsequent occupation, even one that comes a century later". Indeed, McCoy draws a parallel between the U.S. "liberation" of the Philippines and the war in Iraq, showing how "both invasions also began with strong support from similar political coalitions of Republican partisans, imperial ideologues, corporate contractors, middle-class patriots, and working-class soldiers"; how both invaded countries suffered a high number of civilian casualties (200,000 in the Philippines, while some estimate over a million in Iraq); how following a quick military victory a long drawn-out "dirty war" of pacification ensued, replete with "clandestine penetration, psychological warfare, disinformation, media manipulation, assassination, and torture" (McCoy, 2009, p. 5). However, the comparison is also telling by contrast. Where Gen. MacArthur pardoned the Filipino head of state and gave his officers "positions under colonial rule," which was essential to the success of the pacification campaign, the Bush administration dissolved the Iraqi government, demobilized the defeated army, and sent them home with their guns (McCoy, 2009, p. 6).

In the five years that followed 9/11, "the Bush administration expanded domestic surveillance with the USA Patriot Act, monitored domestic communications in defiance of U.S. law, and legal-ized CIA psychological torture under the Military Commissions Act of 2006" (McCoy, 2009, p. 7). De Genova (2010, p. 616) argues that what we are witnessing now is "the institutionalization [and globalization] of the Homeland Security State and the normalization of the antiterrorist 'state of emergency'". What the author also highlights is the exceptionalist discourse in which the war has been framed, one that exceptionalizes the situation into a new era with new legal challenges that requires the state to deal with people who "do not abide by any law," leading to the necessity to not constrain policing with legality and so requiring preventive detention without due process, and ultimately aerial strikes and assassinations (De Genova, 2010, pp. 618–619). With respect to exceptionalism, some argue that it is endemic to empire; the American empire is a manifestation of the rule, as empires necessarily create states of exception, creating a dichotomy between their rationalizing discourse and universal laws, and the situations they create (Stoler & Bond, 2006). De Genova argues that American self-perceived exceptionalism is two-faceted: it perceives the U.S as being exceptional, the land of freedom, opportunity, and inalienable rights, "anointed by divine providence"; but it is also an exception in distinction with the rest of the world—it claims to be unlike previous European colonial empires, having liberated itself from Britain and established a land of freedom, and has a profound sense of its "intrinsic goodness," its uniqueness, and mission to promote its "exemplary model" to the world (De Genova, 2010, p. 619). U.S. exceptionalism, positing a "new era of enlightenment and emancipation at the apex of human history," puts it in competition with Europe in asserting this hegemony and justifies its "'anti-colonial' imperialism"—thus, within its mythology, any moment of genocide, brutality, or colonization, is deemed an anomaly within its righteous quest (De Genova, 2010, pp. 619–621).

De Genova uses the events after hurricane Katrina, and the ensuing abandonment of African Americans, left to their own devices, to reveal the conceit behind the Homeland Security State's "safeguarding and protecting the U.S. population from cataclysmic emergency," highlighting the profoundly white supremacist component of the war on terror as being determinately focused on targeting immigrants, and racializing Muslims as being all suspect (De Genova, 2010, p. 626; also see Noel in this volume). The author calls the "Muslim Question" the constant conundrum of sorting out the good from the bad Muslim, part of the necessity to associate a culprit and enemy to the "amorphous and borderless war", noting that "detentions" have been the hallmark of the Homeland Security State (De Genova, 2010, pp. 626–629). Furthermore, De Genova makes the argument that the "good versus bad Muslim" discourse can be embedded within a wider "friend versus enemy" one that universalizes the conflict where anything but "submission and conformity to the reign of the global regime of capital accumulation" and to "civilization" is considered a potential terrorist threat (De Genova, 2010, p. 630). Thus the empire's multiculturalist discourse is one of assimilation reminiscent of its own domestic "melting pot" (that, like all colonial ventures, dangle the carrot of inclusion while perpetuating an exclusionist structure) (see Berman, 2004; Comaroff, 1998; Mamdani, 2001). Indeed, this "civilization" is couched in a teleological narrative of terrorists being an impediment to the ineluctable march toward social perfection. American history becomes universal history, and the world becomes a Western frontier to be conquered and assimilated as part of America's own civilizing mission. Within this drama, constructing "terrorists" as fundamentally evil and unassimilable carries some terrible consequences as to the value of their life (De Genova, 2010, pp. 630–634). In this light, the failure of the Obama administration to release those Guantanamo prisoners that have been cleared of suspicion takes on frightening connotations.

Spaces that Matter

I would like to close this discussion by highlighting the extent to which the structural environment has a profound influence on human behavior, and how decontextualized, and indeed exceptionalized spaces, carry with them profound potential for violence, abuse, and exploitation, by setting the above arguments against a social experiment that was conducted in the 1970s. In 1971, Haney, Banks, and Zimbardo (1973) decided to replicate a prison environment in the basement of Stanford University in order to test popular assumptions that attributed prison violence and corruption to the moral failings of "bad seeds" rather than to the structural disciplinary environment. To do this they assembled a group of 24 Caucasian undergraduate students with no previous acquaintance, all from the same socio-economic background, and picked precisely for their apparent physical and mental health stability. The group was arbitrarily divided into guards and prisoners, with the guards given very limited instructions to maintain order and prepare for such eventualities as prisoner escape. While the experiment was scheduled to last for two weeks, and despite the fact that guards and prisoners were essentially free to interact as they pleased, it had to be brought to an end after six days, due to the daily escalation of harassment and abuse.

The authors reported some particularly striking findings. For one, they observed a "distressing...ease with which sadistic behavior could be elicited in individuals who were not 'sadistic types' and the frequency with which acute emotional breakdowns could occur in men selected precisely for their emotional stability" (Haney, Banks, and Zimbardo, 1973, p. 89). They also found that their experiment added to Milgram's demonstration that evil deeds could be operated through "powerful social forces" rather than by "evil men" by showing that even without the immediate presence of a legitimating authority figure, "situational variables [had the power] to shape complex social behavior" (Mischel quoted in Haney et al., 1973, p. 90). Furthermore, the experimenters also found that harassment was greater when guards thought they were not being observed, and that aggression continued to escalate even after "most prisoners had stopped resisting and prisoner deterioration had become visibly obvious to them," which occurred visibly after the second day as prisoners began having emotional breakdowns (Haney et al., 1973, p. 92). This escalation of harassment was justified by saying they were "playing the role". This should cause us to ask how far must the situation escalate before individuals manage to escape the story line.

The ability to give orders rather than negotiate proved to be "exhilarating" for the guards: "the use of power was self-aggrandising and self-perpetuating. The guard power, derived initially from an arbitrary label, was intensified whenever there was any perceived threat from the prisoners and this new level subsequently became the baseline from which further hostility and harassment would begin" (Haney et al., 1973, p. 94). The most hostile guards "became role models whose behavior was emulated by other members of the shift....Not to be tough and arrogant was to be seen as a sign of weakness by the guards," and even those who did not engage in the spiral of aggression did not intervene in any way (Haney et al., 1973, p. 94). Rights were virtually instantly redefined as privileges, "constructive activities...were arbitrarily canceled," basic functions such as eating or sleeping were qualified as rewards—"in a world where men are either powerful or powerless, everyone learns to despise the lack of power in others and in oneself" (Haney et al., 1973, p. 94), and so this relationship to power is reproduced, as the powerless seek to exact power where they can. When the experiment was terminated, some guards were reluctant to leave the experiment, having come to enjoy their situation. "Acting authoritatively can be fun. Power can be a great pleasure" remarked one of the guards (Haney et al., 1973, p. 88). Another remarkable finding was that even between themselves the prisoners preserved their roles rather than express their individuality, and that they accepted and adopted the guard's negative attitude towards them and reproduced them with each other. Lastly, it is interesting to note the authors' observation that it is the arbitrary nature of the guards' repressive behavior that had the most deleterious effect on the prisoners and induced inaction and passivity, "since their behavior did not seem to have any contingent relationship to environmental consequences" (Haney et al., 1973, pp. 95–96).

While these findings occurred in a highly controlled environment, and also perhaps because of it, some important insights can be drawn. Writing four decades later, Reimann and Zimbardo (2011) found the principle lessons to be about deindividuation—where individuals are being perceived as anonymous, lacking personal identity, and have a reduced sense of personal accountability—and dehumanization—where "one person considers others to be excluded from the moral order of being a human being". Dehumanization is accompanied by disgust, contempt, and "by a tendency to explain others' behavior in terms of one's own desires rather than cognitive states" (Reimann and Zimbardo , 2011, p. 177).

Alkadry and Witt (2009), in their exploration of the underlying factors that made the events at Abu Ghraib possible, explore Arendt's "administrative evil" and its legitimizing orders, and Zimbardo's Stanford Experiment with its situational psychological transformation, but find that there are wider forces at play in the normalization of torture and gradual demonization and dehumanizing of the Arab other. Hollywood (since the 1980s at least, with hundreds of productions that have caricatured Arabs as the evil other); political and religious leaders; and, the media in general, have all contributed to shaping a cultural environment that has led to the current crisis. In the authors' opinion, the very fact that torture and its definition are being debated shows how torture has moved from the background of unconditional taboo to the relative foreground, and points to the moral degradation, and resetting of the ethical framework by which individuals judge each other.

Conclusion

This perpetual shaping and reshaping of our normative environ-ment, and the consequences it has on how we construct ourselves and our relationship with the world around us, has been the cen-tral insight that my research into empire has provided me and that I have tried to convey in this admittedly disjointed narrative. The purpose of the lengthy examination of the social, political, and economic transformations that led up to Britain's New Imperial-ism, and to the American empire that followed, was to show that much of our current situation, far from being exceptional, can be found to be rooted in earlier processes that have followed a con-tinuous accretion up to the present. Not only do they highlight the persistent fallaciousness of the economic rhetoric we are served, but more importantly it reveals a subtle and insidious ideological shift toward the understanding of structural causality as individ-ual moral failure. It is the degree to which the environment, in its widest possible meaning (physical, institutional, semiotic, etc), im-pacts our cognitive processes, altering our ontological boundaries, that I have sought to suggest. The actions of an empire are never only those of one actor acting upon another, nor even those of a multitude of actors acting upon each other—they are better under-stood, in this perspective, as those of an actor acting upon himself. That is to say that the world an empire shapes is the world it has to contend with, both materially and ontologically. It is also to say that the rhetoric necessary to justify the subjugation of a people, be it abroad or at home, and be that domination military, eco-nomic, or cultural, insidiously becomes the epistemological toolkit that gradually redefines the way reality is apprehended and un-derstood. It is seen in the higher echelons of power with unimagi-native leaders painting a world with no other alternatives and endorsing ever more repressive and paranoid measures, and in the military excesses of soldiers responding to their culture's dehu-manizing subtext. It highlights the fragility of the normative envi-ronment, the flexibility humans have in adapting to it, and the responsibility we bear in shaping the material and hermeneutic world we live in. It also highlights that the first step in having an enemy is to define him as such.

References

Alkadry, M. G., & Witt, M. T. (2009). Abu Ghraib and the Normalization of Torture and Hate. *Public Integrity*, 11(2), 135–153.

Babones, S. (2012). The Death of the Great American Middle Class. *Steve Keen's Debtwatch*, February 28.

http://www.debtdeflation.com/blogs/2012/02/28/the-death-of-the-great-american-middle-class/

Berman, B. J. (2004). A Palimpsest of Contradictions: Ethnicity, Class, and Politics in Africa. The International Journal of African Historical Studies, 37(1), 13–31.

Book TV. (2012). In Depth with Author and Journalist Chris Hedges. *C-SPAN*, January 1.

http://www.c-span.org/Events/In-Depth-with-Author-and-Journalist-Chris-Hedges/10737426679-1/

Brown, A. D.; Kouri, N.; & Hirst, W. (2012). Memory's Malleability: Its Role in Shaping Collective Memory and Social Identity. *Frontiers in Psychology*, 3.

http://www.ncbi.nlm.nih.gov/pmc/articles/PMC3402138/

Cain, P. J., & Hopkins, A. G. (1986). Gentlemanly Capitalism and British Expansion Overseas I. The Old Colonial System, 1688–1850. *The Economic History Review*, 39(4), 501–525.

————— . (1987). Gentlemanly Capitalism and British Expansion Overseas II: New Imperialism, 1850–1945. *The Economic History Review*, 40(1), 1–26.

Chomsky, N. (1998). A Century Later. *Peace Review*, 10(3), 313–320.

————— . (1999). Domestic Terrorism: Notes on the State System of Oppression. *New Political Science*, 21(3), 303–324.

Comaroff, J. L. (1998). Reflections on the Colonial State, in South Africa and Elsewhere: Factions, Fragments, Facts and Fictions. *Social Identities*, 4(3), 321–361.

De Genova, N. (2010). Antiterrorism, Race, and the New Frontier: American Exceptionalism, Imperial Multiculturalism, and the Global Security State. *Identities*, 17(6), 613–640.

Foster, J. B., & McChesney, R. W. (2012). *The Endless Crisis: How Monopoly-Finance Capital Produces Stagnation and Upheaval from the USA to China*. New York, NY: Monthly Review Press.

Haney, C.; Banks, C.; & Zimbardo, P. (1973). Interpersonal Dynamics in a Simulated Prison. *International Journal of Criminology and Psychology*, 1, 69–97.

Harvey, D. (2005). *The New Imperialism*. New York, NY: Oxford University Press.

Limerick, P. (2012). The American West as the Essential Laboratory for the Study of Dependence on and Resentment of the Federal Government. Rediscovering Government Launch Conference, Historical Role of Goverment Panel, March 28.

http://www.rooseveltinstitute.org/sites/all/files/Patty%20Limerick_0.pdf

Lutz, C. (2011). Catherine Lutz: "Magical Thinking" and the Costs of War. *Radio Open Source with Christopher Lydon*, April 10.

http://www.radioopensource.org/catherine-lutz-magical-thinking-and-the-costs-of-war/

Mamdani, M. (2001). Beyond Settler and Native as Political Identities: Overcoming the Political Legacy of Colonialism. *Comparative Studies in Society & History*, 43(4), 651–664.

McCaull, J. (1976). Pursuit of Property. *Environment*, 18(6), 17–31.

——————— . (2009). *Policing America's Empire*. Madison, WI: University of Wisconsin Press.

McCoy, A. W., & Scarano, F. A. (2009). *Colonial Crucible*. Madison, WI: University of Wisconsin Press.

Noam Chomsky Videos. (2011) Imperial Dangers: Then and Now (Full Speech) [Video file].
http://www.youtube.com/watch?v=nUDVhPHSWVo

Novak, W. J. (2008). The Myth of the "Weak" American State. *American Historical Review*, 113(3), 752–772.

Perlstein, R. (2006). Thunder on the Right: The Roots of Conservative Victory in the 1960s. *OAH Magazine of History*, 20(5), 24–27.

——————— . (2011). Inside the GOP's Fact-Free Nation. *Mother Jones*, May-June.
http://www.motherjones.com/politics/2011/04/history-political-lying

Pollin, R. (2007). Economic Prospects: Global Outsourcing and the U.S. Working Class. *New Labor Forum*, 16(1), 122–125.

Reimann, M., & Zimbardo, P. G. (2011). The Dark Side of Social Encounters: Prospects for a Neuroscience of Human Evil. *Journal of Neuroscience, Psychology, & Economics*, 4(3), 174–180.

Soederberg, S. (2001). The Emperor's New Suit: The New International Financial Architecture as a Reinvention of the Washington Consensus. *Global Governance*, 7(4), 453–467.

——————— . (2005). The Transnational Debt Architecture and Emerging Markets: The Politics of Paradoxes and Punishment. *Third World Quarterly*, 26(6), 927–949.

Somers, M. R., & Block, F. (2005). From Poverty to Perversity: Ideas, Markets, and Institutions Over 200 Years of Welfare Debate. *American Sociological Review*, 70(2), 260–287.

Steinmetz, G. (2005). Return to Empire: The New U.S. Imperialism in Comparative Historical Perspective. *Sociological Theory*, 23(4), 339–367.

Stoler, A., & Bond, D. (2006). Refractions Off Empire: Untimely Comparisons in Harsh Times. *Radical History Review*, (95), 93–107.

Strange, S. (1992). States, Firms and Diplomacy. *International Affairs (Royal Institute of International Affairs*, 68(1), 1–15.

——————— . (1999). The Westfailure System. *Review of International Studies*, 25(3), 345–354.

Taibbi, M. (2013). Everything is Rigged: The Biggest Price-Fixing Scandal Ever. *Rolling Stone*, April 25.
http://www.rollingstone.com/politics/news/everything-is-rigged-the-

biggest-financial-scandal-yet-20130425

Tilly, C. (1982). Warmaking and Statemaking as Organized Crime. Center for Research on Social Organization, University of Michigan.

U.S. Senate (1976). Final Report of the Select Committee to Study Governmental Operations with Respect to Intelligence Activities. Washington, DC: U.S. Senate.

http://web.archive.org/web/20101017040843/http://www.raven1.net/co inteldocs/churchfinalreportIIb.htm

Ware, N. J. (1935). *Labor in Modern Industrial Society*. Boston: D. C. Heath and Company.

CHAPTER TWO

The Masculine Empire: A Gendered Analysis of Modern American Imperialism

Nicolas Pas

"The Orient was Orientalized not only because it was discovered to be 'Oriental' in all those ways considered commonplace by an average nineteenth-century European, but also because it *could be*—that is, submitted to being—*made* Oriental. There is very little consent to be found, for example, in the fact that Flaubert's encounter with an Egyptian courtesan produced a widely influential model of the Oriental woman; she never spoke of herself, she never represented her emotions, presence or history. *He* spoke for and represented her. He was foreign, comparatively wealthy, male, and these were historical facts of domination that allowed him not only to possess [her] physically but to speak for her and tell his readers in what way she was 'typically Oriental'....[This relationship] stands for the pattern of relative strength between East and West, and the discourse about the Orient that it enabled". (Said, 1979, p. 5–6)

It is my claim that modern American empire-building adopts traditionally heteronormative objectification in affirming its national power. This system acts to project dominant micro-familial ideology that is developed at home, overseas on the level of nations. Thus, I will argue that modern American empire-building assumes and constructs a narrative of heteronormative domestic

patriarchy in foreign affairs—serving to empower the home country and its military while simultaneously effeminizing the host
country to rationalize its successful heterosexual objectification
and subsequent domination. This objectification results in Afghan
and Iraqi citizens being perceived as a homogenous entity rather
than a group of individuals or identities which parallel our own. I
will demonstrate this through a gendered discussion of the "War
on Terror" in Afghanistan and Iraq.

First, it is important for me to contextualize the approach to
imperialism being used throughout this paper. While imperialism
arguably manifests in myriad forms and intersects relations of
dominance, power, and general control, for the purposes of my argument I will be focusing on one of the two dualistic descriptions of
capitalist imperialism that David Harvey (2003) outlines. I will be
discussing imperialism as "a contradictory fusion of the 'politics of
state and empire'" —more specifically, "imperialism as a distinc-
tively political project on the part of actors whose power is based in
command of a territory and a capacity to mobilize its human and
natural resources towards political, economic, and military ends"
(Harvey, 2003, p. 25).[1]

Drawing on Laura Mulvey's psychoanalysis of male power and
female objectification— "an idea of woman stands as lynch pin to
the system: it is her lack [of a phallus] that produces the phallus
as a symbolic presence" (1990, p. 57) —this conception of women's
lack of a phallus as standing in as a symbol for man's phallic
power, although taken out of context and intended to be psycho-
analytical, can alternatively and in a much more literal sense be
applied to our discussion of American imperial power. What the
Middle East supposedly lacks becomes a symbol for American superiority. In defining a masculine American imperial identity, ideologies and practices viewed as antithetical or "un-American" are
examined and systematically "othered". American imperial identity is defined as masculine and superior simply through the feminization of the Middle East. In relation to Laura Mulvey's
psychoanalysis of the objectified woman, we can argue that the
Middle East stands in as the lynch pin to the system of American
Imperialism—it is the lack of American ideals and notions of basic
inferiority in Afghanistan and Iraq which stands as a symbol for
American superiority. American Imperialism and American identity in and of itself becomes defined by that which it is not—
Middle Eastern and effeminate.[2]

This relationship adopts a gendered narrative which will be outlined throughout the entirety of this essay and can be further tied into Mulvey's language of "lack" —where a lack of American ideology in the Middle East acts to fetishize these ideologies in America and American foreign policy. American foreign policy in Afghanistan and Iraq is developed on the basis that individuals in the Middle East lack democracy, freedom, and civilization; this lack becomes a marker of Western superiority, civil modernity, and the illusion (or delusion) of "freedom". In other words the "oppressed" Muslim other stands in as a lynch pin in this system – Afghan and Iraqi oppression comes to signify American freedom and democracy. This perception of the "oppressed other" provides a legitimizing narrative for the current civilizing mission that has been obscured within a rhetorical framework that utilizes the altruism of terms like the "humanitarian intervention" or "peacebuilding operations".

Thus, the physical penetration and figurative insemination of Iraq and Afghanistan is validated in that it is claimed to result in the birth of what these nations apparently lack; democracy, freedom, and civilization. Furthermore, this penetrative, reproductive, and fundamentally heterosexual relationship can be reaffirmed in the statement, "the birth pangs of a new Middle East" made by Condoleezza Rice during a conference in 2006 to find a "lasting solution" to the conflict between Lebanon and Israel (Beale, 2006). This term has now been used in countless journalistic news headlines documenting the invasions in the Middle East by the U.S.

Since these ideologies of democracy, freedom, and civilization act as markers of the difference between America and the Middle East and thus the supposed moral superiority of America, it would be antagonistic to the imperial project to destabilize the status quo. Rather, the dominant perception of the Middle East as lacking those ideologies which America supposedly upholds must be maintained if the imperial project is to continue undetected. The American public needs to be reminded of what defines their citizenship, their national identity, and their freedom; this is done through reminders of what Afghanistan and Iraq lack—they lack these fundamental ideologies that allow for a supposedly "free" America. Thus the oppressed Islamic "other" needs to be continuously acknowledged as a reminder of what it means to be a "free" American and keep the public's eyes off of the imperial project. This is done through "peacebuilding operations" and "liberation" projects which act to feminize these countries, further warranting and rendering their penetration heterosexual and thus made "safe".[3]

Gendering Imperialism, Effeminizing the Subordinated Other

In understanding the gendering and heteronormative nature of modern U.S. imperialism it is important to acknowledge the implication of gender and sexuality in the processes of empire-building throughout history, specifically discussing European colonial pursuits. Within the British empire of the nineteenth-century a pattern of heteronormative familial domesticity was created where "colonizers and colonized were seen as members of one imperial family" (Webster, 1998, p. 27). The colonies were depicted as the daughters of England; the colonized thus became the children of the empire, with "England as their motherland or mother country" (Webster, 1998, p. 27). Furthering this relationship of domestic patriarchy on the level of nations, the British monarchs were often imagined to be the fathers or mothers of this family (Webster, 1998, p. 27). The micro-familial household thus became synonymous with the nation itself, and man's position in this became well-defined. He was the protector and emperor of his family within the domestic sphere, he was also to maintain and protect his empire on the level of nations if he was to be considered a true and masculine "citizen". The home and the nation became tantamount and man's power within both was reaffirmed. The nuances of this familial relationship can be observed through an examination of Britannia, the ancient name for Great Britain itself along with the female personification of Britain, an icon developed in 1688 (Major, 2012, p. 7). This female figure holds a shield and a trident and is undoubtedly meant to embody the strength of the nation. Thus the message is apparent yet strangely paradoxical. While the men colonize overseas, the women remain in the motherland, nurturing and protecting the nation's youth—the empire's future militants. It is the women's position not only to nurture the nation's young, but also to cultivate and engrain notions of nationality within these young, producing strong soldiers and national citizens to maintain the British Empire. Although she is not to be a part of the public sphere or the imperial pursuit she is absolutely embedded in the process.

Figure 2.1: Britannia

Statue of Britannia on top of the National Armada Memorial on
Plymouth Hoe (photograph by Nilfanion, Wikimedia Commons).

Figure 2.2: An Imperial Marriage

Britannia with the British Lion and Uncle Sam with the American Bald Eagle on a World War I poster (source: Wikimedia Commons).

The colonial penetration of India by Britain as a fundamentally masculine pursuit relying on the racialization, effeminization, and ultimate "othering" of the colonized people as justification, is also argued by Krishnaswamy (1998). This can be read in conjuncture with the aforementioned discussion of the feminization of the Middle East for the systematic empowerment of the American empire. Krishnaswamy discusses the invasion of India as a "homosocial pursuit" whereby the British men were seen as the ultimate embodiment of masculinity whilst the Indian men were viewed by the British as effeminate—often described in terms of homosexual identities which served to rationalize colonial dominance.[4] Indian culture was effeminized in a multitude of ways, the most pertinent to my topic being through the use of religion—with Hinduism being seen as ecstatic, improper, irrational and feminine—and rape—with "metaphoric and disguised images of...invasion, possession, regression, and decline" (Krishnaswamy, 1998, p. 25) (terms which he argues represent white male penetration). Krishnaswamy outlines the use of Indian women as a legitimating mechanism for British colonialism. Indian women were "cast as the hapless victims of barbaric Indian patriarchy" (1998, p. 17) whilst Indian males were seen as incapable of achieving the British "chivalric ideal of manhood" in protecting their female counterparts. Their failure to stand up to British standards of chivalrous masculinity as read through the eyes of the British public resulted in their effeminization.[5] Krishnaswamy (1998) argues that the status of women is used as a measure of civil society but that British interests lay more in the effeminization of Indian men than the emancipation of women as it was this effeminization that rationalized their penetration.

Sexuality and Empire-Building

The history of empire building is not free of gendered and sexual paradigms. Now we must outline how these same processes have been applied to the invasions and occupations of Iraq and Afghanistan in the maintenance of contemporary U.S. imperialism. I would argue that American standards of masculinity have adopted these same narratives of chivalry. Connell (1995) aims to understand contemporary Western masculinities through the dissemination of former structures of masculinity (and gender as a whole) in the context of global empires and global capitalist economy. As Connell explains, "European/American masculinities were deeply implicated in the world-wide violence through which European/American culture became dominant" (1995, p. 186). Connell begins by noting what is most obvious, and thus most overlooked and taken for granted: "Empire was a gendered enterprise from the start, initially an outcome of the segregated men's occupations of soldiering and sea trading" (1995, p. 187).

Archetypes of masculinity have often been those of "men of the frontier" and thus Connell argues there is an inherent connection between the construction of masculinity, global violence, and empire-building. Connell states that these men of the frontier were possibly one of the first groups to "become defined as a masculine cultural type in the modern sense" (1995, p. 187). Therefore, "masculinities are not only shaped by the process of imperial expansion. They are active in that process and help to shape it" (Connell, 2005, p. 185). Furthermore, it is evident that the military can also be seen as a homosocial[6] masculine space on a global scale. That is to say that military force in and of itself is arguably inherently masculine—whether American or not. I am aware that my description of the military as masculine is guilty of reading masculinity through a Western lens—that however, is not my intention, as much as I am in fact focusing on Western masculinity. If we engage Connell's statement on a literal plane, rather than theoretical, the statistics speak for the positive relationship between men and the military globally. Throughout the history of men's conscription, millions of men have been conscripted to fight in wars across the world whilst women have been excluded (Benatar, 2012, p. 27).[7] However, my choice to assign the narrative of "masculinity" to the U.S. military on a theoretical level calls for more than a statistical analysis of men's inclusion in war.

9/11, Emasculation, and the Cowboy Rides Again

If we choose to accept Connell's argument that masculinity is inherently intertwined with imperial force, then we can see how threats to the American empire can be read as threats of emasculation. Segal (2008) interprets the attacks on the Twin Towers on September 11th as being richly symbolic in its potential to signify emasculation:

> "[the] reaction everywhere played upon images of the event as the consummate symbolic emasculation of America's phallic power. As commentators from both the Islamic and the

Western world have noted, the spectacular 'triumph' of that event was adroitly staged both to assuage the sense of inferiority and injustice of a deeply divided Muslim world, as well as to ignite its anger against the US-Western military onslaught certain to follow....Launching his 'war on terrorism', George W. Bush often presented himself in army uniform, strutting an invincible American masculinity". (Segal, 2008, p. 31)[8]

This masculine retaliation to the emasculating wound of 9/11 is demonstrated in Bush's comments to Tony Blair's communications director after Blair agreed to contribute British troops to the war in Iraq: "Your man's got cojones" (Woodward, 2004, p. 178).[9] Clearly, in retaliation to the attacks on 9/11, masculine force was enacted—America needed to reaffirm its patriarchal domination over the effeminized Middle East. We can witness the direct use of masculinity in the types of military representation used. In a lecture at Concordia University by Anne McClintock (2013) she discussed the "Indianization" of the Middle East. McClintock draws parallels between America's colonial genocide and displacement of Native Americans and the current invasion of Afghanistan and Iraq. In this analysis we see the recurring image of the cowboy. In a multitude of photo shoots set up by the American press just prior to the "war on terror" we see the American militant on horseback, dressed in the garb of a colonial cowboy. The cowboy is an image that comes up time and time again in American military imagery and can be reiterated in the naming of "Operation Geronimo," a Native American name adopted for Osama Bin Laden's manhunt (McClintock, 2013). The cowboy, a historical and fundamentally American symbol of masculinity and of man on the frontier is blatantly embodied in the militarized and imperial reaction to the emasculating wound of 9/11. The American military stands in as dualistically symbolic—not only symbolizing America's imperial power, but as such symbolizing the masculine narrative which this imperial power adopts.

Security Feminism

Although it could be argued that current ideas of traditional male sex roles seem to be relaxing within the American metropolis itself, Connell argues this is the product of the world capitalist order where the enlightenment project is now the export of Western gender ideology. He argues that the "oppression" of women in the

Islamic world is simply a reaction to Western gender order; the Middle East is "pursuing a gender politics through the same gestures as an anti-colonial politics" (2005, p. 200). Although I am hesitant to adopt Connell's language of oppression, the current war in Afghanistan and Iraq has time and time again been justified under the pretext that Islam is oppressive to women. Not only are the doctrines of the Quran themselves seen as oppressive, but so are the severe relations of patriarchal power which these doctrines purportedly enable. The burqa-clad woman has become the poster-child for the "war against terror".[10] This acts to further feminize Afghanistan and Iraq both as nations and on the level of individual citizens.

This situation is analogous to Krishnaswamy's (1998) discussion of the effeminization of British India—the focus on Afghan and Iraqi women as the helpless victims of oppression pits their male counterparts as barbaric and lacking the American ideal of chivalrous masculinity. The Afghan and Iraqi man does not stand up to American standards of masculinity—thus making him feminine—and simultaneously stands as a point of negation in the development of an American masculinity. Again, America is made out to be morally modern while the Middle-East skulks in the shadow of civilization as the feminized "other". American civil modernity is professed in negation of Islamic women's perceived oppression. Not only does this give Americans a false perception of civil liberty and equality at home, it further perpetuates the issue which foreign policy is claiming to resolve. Nesiah (2012) discusses the recent emergence of "security feminism" in American foreign policy which claims to "heighten visibility and significance of gender issues," effectively creating a coalition between feminism and counterterrorism. She argues that this is not simply a tactic to advance nationalism and militarization but in actuality is an attempt to highlight vulnerability by problematically pitting the female as the only victim of counterterrorism efforts. This effectively fetishizes the Muslim woman—the war becomes about her. In this process the host country is also feminized and the American heterosexual pursuit becomes about gallantly "saving" the Muslim woman from Islam. While America strives to save the Muslim woman from her alleged theological oppression she is effectively put on the front lines (see Hanifi, 2009).

Female Engagement and Masculinized American Women

Krishnaswamy discusses early English feminists in British India, explaining that these women empowered themselves by adopting "the secluded Indian woman as the object of their own unique female Salvationist project..." (1998, p. 36). These women embodied a "contradictory combination of sexual subordination and racial domination" (1998, p. 37) in that they were in a position of colonizer but also subordinate to men within the patriarchal British Empire. Similarly, the pro-war American feminist can be considered within this same lens. Take for example the more recent involvement of Female Engagement Teams (FETs) in Afghanistan and Iraq. These women are deployed to these nations specifically to gain access to information from the "other" 50% of the Afghan peoples—women. Their job is to provide these women with "autonomy" and act as a mediator in giving them a voice. These FETs are also to engage in comfortable conversation with children who are involved in nearly all aspects of the community and are the "Afghan future". If these groups can be targeted at a young age there is hope that they will not become involved in the insurgency in their later years (Stanton, 2011). While it is the case that these individuals' voices will now be heard, we need to ask "by whom?"

Figure 2.3: Women's Day in Afghanistan

Afghan women gathered by U.S. troops in order to celebrate International Women's Day at the Ministry of Culture and Information, March 8. (Photo by U.S. Air Force 1st Lt. Nicholas Mercurio)

Figure 2.4: Female Engagement Team, Afghanistan

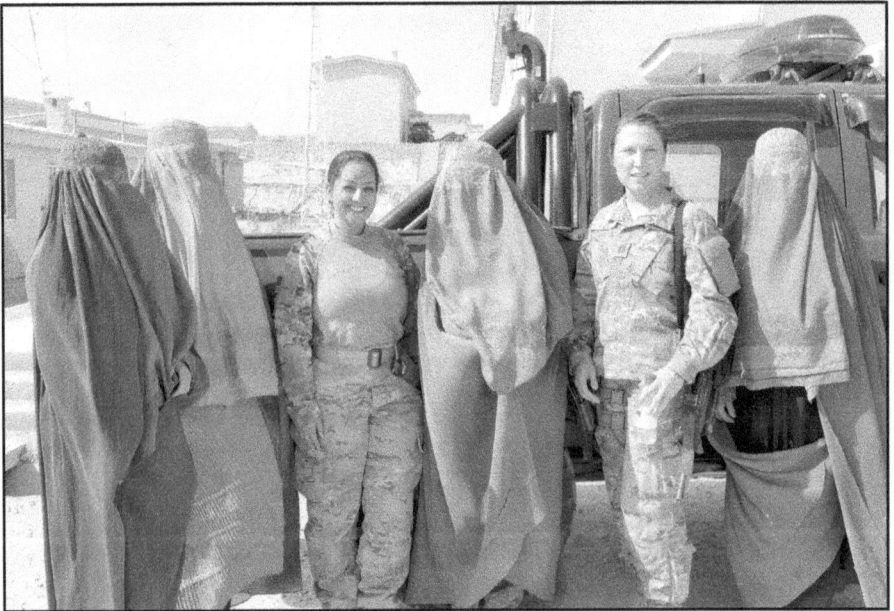

U.S. Army Maj. Maria Rodriguez and Air Force Capt. Leslee Kane lead female engagement teams in Afghanistan. (U.S. Army photo by Pvt. Andreka Johnson, 1st Stryker Brigade Combat Team, 25th Infantry Division Public Affairs)

In conjunction with this, it is important that we challenge the dynamics of power and oppression which are involved in these processes of "emancipation". As in Krishnaswamy's discussion of British colonial women these American FETs and female troops' position in Afghanistan and Iraq becomes enigmatic. These women occupy a position of racial and perceived Western superiority over the Islamic "others" who they purport to be liberating. Even their physical presence in this foreign land serves to draw attention to the power which these women have over their Middle Eastern counterparts. As previously discussed, the U.S. military is ostensibly invading Iraq and Afghanistan on the basis of these nations' antiquated civil and moral ideologies, although not directly put this way in popular media. This makes evident that a hierarchy has been developed between Western and Eastern values—the U.S. army, including these women are there to aid in the emancipation and enlightenment of this society. American women occupy these nations on the basis of their assumed civil superiority; this not only puts them in a position of power over the women they are attempting to emancipate, but even more so over the local men they are "saving" these women from. This acts to further feminize Afghan and Iraqi men now that American women can be read as more chivalrous than their Middle Eastern male counterparts. In negation of these feminized Afghan and Iraqi men, these American women become masculinized. The masculinization of these female troops can be further witnessed in the case of Abu Ghraib where a female soldier was photographed standing with naked, male, and Middle Eastern torture victims on a leash. McClintock (2013) draws parallels to this type of torture and rape—a show of masculine power. It could be argued that the female photographed in Abu Ghraib took on a narrative of masculine power.

Figure 2.5: Iraqi Women and Children Wait for Food

Iraqi women and children wait to receive food aid during Operation Iron H1115 in Muhallah 755, Fedaliyah, eastern Baghdad, on Nov. 12, 2008. (U.S. Army photo by Staff Sgt. James Selesnick.)

Figure 2.6: An Iraqi Woman Pleads

An Iraqi woman yells at U.S. Army Spc. William Gregory, as he pulls security outside of a house during a combined cordon and search with the Iraqi police in the West Rashid district of Baghdad, Iraq, June 26, 2007. (U.S. Army photo by Sgt. Tierney Nowland)

Figure 2.7: Iraqi Man on a Woman's Leash

U.S. Army photo from Abu Ghraib prison in Iraq showing Pvt. Lynndie England holding a leash attached to a prisoner collapsed on the floor, known to the guards as "Gus".

Figure 2.8: Woman's Underwear on an Iraqi Man's Head

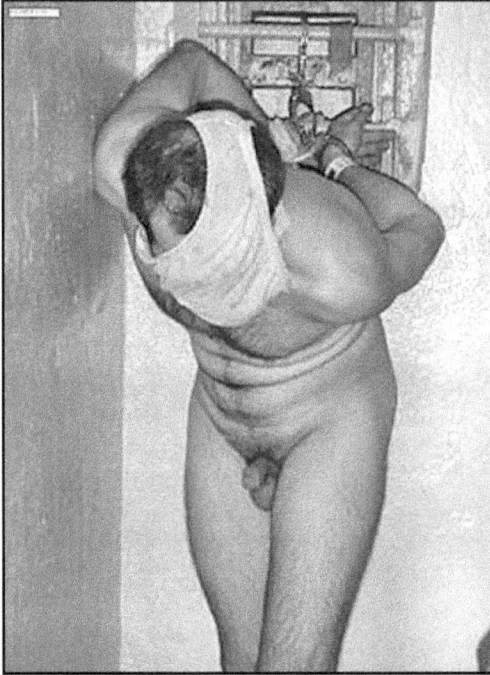

Top: Another of the infamous leaked photographs from Abu Ghraib. This man has been stripped naked, with his head covered by a woman's panty.

Bottom: Lynndie England points her imaginary gun down at the penis of one of the Iraqi detainees.

Figure 2.9: U.S. Woman's "Gun" Pointed at an Iraqi Man's Penis

The Liberating Subordinated American Woman Soldier

Making this situation paradoxical is the position in which American women occupy in relation to their male colleagues. *The Invisible War* is a 2012 film which attempts to uncover American military rape that has been shielded from the public since the "war on terror" began.[11] The statistics are damning—female military personnel are more likely to be raped by a fellow soldier than to be killed in enemy fire, 500,000 women have been assaulted in the American military by their peers.[12] Of these reported sexual assault cases only 8% have been prosecuted in the military, and "only 2% result in convictions" (Barklow, Ziering, & Dick, 2012). This is a very drastic and violent example of these women's oppression in relation to their male counterparts. This is further exemplified in the cases of female soldiers dying of dehydration in the middle of the night for fear of being raped on their trip to latrines (Benedict, 2007). If females report rape they are often met with a culture of punishment—they would be considered "incapable traitors" and would face "rumors, resentment, and blame" (Benedict, 2007). While these women presume to emancipate Islamic women from their gendered oppression they are facing the same symptoms of oppression from fellow troops.[13] Furthermore, while these women are being accepted into the armed forces they are simultaneously being excluded in that they must face fear and anxiety during duty. It is situations like these which make the entanglement of masculinity, violence,[14] and masculine power within the military undeniably evident.

Girls' Schools: The New Front Line

Outlined in an American Congressional Research Service Report (CRS Report) entitled *Assistance to Afghan and Iraqi Women: Issues for Congress* (Armanios & Margesson, 2004) the need for a focus on women and children is explicated. The authors state that aiding in the liberation of women and children along with the development of democracy in Afghanistan and Iraq requires a strong focus on women and children's education. The intentions for foreign policy, along with the wealth of NGOs in both Afghanistan and Iraq, specify education and schools for women and children as the top priority (Armanios & Margesson, 2004). This is all executed in full knowledge of the Taliban's opposition to public—and specifically women's—education which has been reported time and time again. The development of these schools has actually become a point of retaliation to the Taliban's ban on public education, a system meant to efface the Taliban's systematic oppression of women and children. While it is not my intention to argue that these groups should remain barred from education, we do need to acknowledge that the U.S.' abrasive approach to gendered equality—that is simply applying American ideals overseas—can actually be seen to cause more harm than good.

During a monologue in *Apocalypse Now* (1979), the character of Col. Kurtz tells of a horrifying scene in the midst of the Vietnam War. A group of American soldiers leave a campsite after inoculating a group of children for polio. A few steps away from the site, an old man chases the soldiers crying. The soldiers follow him back to find a pile of children's arms at the site of the inoculation (Woodman, 2003, p. 51). The Viet Cong soldiers had amputated the arms of the inoculated children as a symbol for the physical removal of both the American soldiers themselves along with the Western values which had been inscribed on the bodies of their youth. While this is a fictional account of brutality in reaction to American infiltration, there can be parallels drawn to this scene. Take for example the multiple acid attacks on women carried out by the Taliban following their loss of power in 2001. Shamsia Husseini recounts her experience of being sprayed in the face with acid on her way to school in Afghanistan by a man who was claimed to be a fundamentalist member of the Taliban. On the same day 11 other female students and four teachers were all sprayed with acid. The New York Times claims that these attacks were the result of the Taliban's battle against the Afghan government and American-led coalition—women and children were banned from schools before the Taliban were overthrown by the American government (Filkins, 2009). In a similar situation we hear of a group of Afghan girls being poisoned at school (Faiez & Vogt, 2012). It was claimed that the Taliban had bribed school faculty and students to spray poison throughout the school and into drinking water, thus causing a large group of girls to fall ill. These are but a few of the attacks on school children and women in reaction to public education by the fundamentalist group. In addition to individuals being assaulted, many teachers and students have been killed and over 200 schools have been reported destroyed, most of which were girls and women's schools (Zada & Santana, 2012). In all of these reports the authors claim that these actions were done in an attempt to keep girls from gaining an education, especially a non-Islamic one: "The Taliban said our school was destroyed because it was not providing an Islamic education" (Palmer, 2009).

Back to our monologue from *Apocalypse Now* (1979): while the bodies of these Taliban women and girls are not being inoculated through vaccinations, it is arguable that through the eyes of the Taliban, their minds are being inoculated by the West. Foreign policy has inadvertently put women and children on the front lines of war. Now we're left to question whether U.S. involvement in the Middle East is liberating or further oppressing these women and children, who are living under the same oppression as before but now in a war zone. Furthermore, the discussions on women and children's lack of educational rights is used to cast *all* Islamic men, rather than the fundamentalist Taliban alone, as being oppressive to women. This further propagates the less than chivalrous, feminine perception of Islamic men.

Evidently there has been a strong emphasis on children's and women's rights in American foreign policy; it is also clear how this focus acts to further effeminize these nations. While the imperial project is unmistakably gendered, I have yet to elucidate how it takes on a heteronormative narrative. Furthering our discussion of children in the war overseas, Edelman (1998) discusses the concept of "political futurity" and how is it molded by the image of the child. She argues that the child represents "reproductive futurism" which privileges heteronormativity and in turn "defines queer identities as embodiments of the death drive" (1998, p. 292). She discusses the ongoing political campaign "we're doing it for the children," and explains that, "we are no more able to conceive of a politics without a fantasy of the future than we are able to conceive of a future without the figure of the child" (Edelman, 1998, p. 290). Not only does this focus on "futurity", or reproduction, overlook queer identities but Edelman argues that within this context queerness actually comes to signify death.

A Queer Empire?

As the child becomes the keystone to a war waged overseas, this effectively occults queer identities. I will further argue that queer identities, although ostensibly "incorporated,"[15] are actually antithetical to the imperial project.

In discussing the inclusion (and simultaneous exclusion) of queer identities in the U.S. army it is important that we consider the Don't Ask Don't Tell policy (DADT) and its repeal. Many qualms were raised preceding discussions of the abolishment of the DADT policy, the most common being that many male soldiers worried that the space that had once been homosocial would become homoerotic upon the open inclusion of gay men within their troops. One of the main defenses of the DADT policy was the privacy which is afforded troops—the unknowing presence of the homosexual "other" while soldiers bathed or changed was thought to keep them safe from the homosexual gaze (Britton & Williams, 1995).

> "While there appears to be room in the military to accommodate the 'male gaze' so long as it is directed at women such a gaze directed at men by men is clearly perceived as threatening and objectifying. The fear seems to be that the gaze of the male homosexual will turn heterosexual men from subjects with desire to objects of desire". (Britton & Williams, 1995, pp. 9–10)

It seems that many had been ignorant of the fact that queer identities were present in the military even under the DADT policy. This fear of the homosexual other, of the homosocial or heterosexual pursuit becoming one intermingled with homoerotic desire is enough for policies like DADT to be implemented in the first place. The homosexual is defined and excluded in the negating of a masculine military force—meanwhile the situation becomes contradictory in that queer identities are technically "permitted" in the military. Perhaps the situation is better elucidated when we acknowledge the exclusion of transgender and intersex individuals on the basis of their physical and mental "unfitness". While the homosexual is permitted within the military a line has still be made in regards to the inclusion of queer identities.

Although the DADT policy has been repealed and homosexual cisgender men and women are legally *tolerated* within the military, there is reason to believe legal tolerance does not mean the same thing as social equality. First and foremost, although these troops are allowed to openly identify, their significant others and families do not receive the same benefits that a heterosexual military family receives. There are many states in America where gay marriage is not recognized—thus these individuals' partners are not seen as legitimate or eligible for these benefits. The Pentagon chooses not to recognize "same-sex couples when allocating medical coverage, housing, travel allowances, and other benefits" (Crary, 2012). Additionally, harassment and discrimination are still occurring towards homosexual individuals within the armed forces, although this harassment has not become worse since the repeal of DADT, it has also not become better (Crary, 2012). The implication of a policy like DADT ever existing implies that queer identities can only exist within the military if their actual existence is unknown. This stands in stark contrast to the lack of attention given to women being sexually assaulted in the military whilst much energy and protest has been put towards excluding queer identities. The American military has adopted a narrative of queer negation further reiterating the heteronormative attitude of American society which is exaggerated within the hypermasculine climate of the military.

The American empire makes itself out to be inclusive and exceptional in regards to queer rights yet it simultaneously excludes and "others" these individuals. Puar argues that,

> "queerness is proffered as a sexually exceptional form of American national sexuality through a rhetoric of sexual modernization that is simultaneously able to castigate the [Muslim] other as homophobic and perverse, and construct the imperialist center as 'tolerant' but sexually, racially, and gendered normal" (2005, p. 122).

In this process there is much focus put on Muslim sexual repression by queer rights groups which focus on the liberation of sexual minorities within the Arab world—this acts as the same projection of barbarity which is adopted in making the American empire seem like a space of freedom and civil modernity. This is paradoxical, however, because for the imperial project to remain heteronormative, masculine, and adopt a narrative of microfamilial patriarchy, queer identities must not become inclusive or normalized. Homoerotic desire threatens the imperial project as it threatens the objectification and homogenization of the "Islamic other"—such desire must therefore be externalized, as in the homoerotic torture of inmates at Abu Ghraib prison. Otherwise, homosexual desire and love may lead to notions of individuality and subjectivity within Afghanistan and Iraq rather than a notion of "the Muslim" as an amalgamated entity. Without this justification of moral "backwardness" or barbarity and the homogenous "other" we begin having to consider the invasion of a land with individuals, identities, and livelihoods—suddenly the war overseas becomes morally apprehensible.

In the inclusion and exclusion of queer identities and women in the military we're left asking "what does equality mean?" In this case it would seem that these groups are reaching equality in oppressing the racial other. It could be argued that the imperial project itself masculinizes those which are systematically "included". In this intricate process of justification and self-identification all things "other" are negated and expunged. The racial other, the woman, and the queer other all stand as symbols of amalgamated "otherness" along with markers of American freedom, liberty, civil modernity, and most of all, masculinity. This familial relationship reminds us of the reproductive futurity necessary both for a thriving empire along with a micro-familial domesticity. Thus the family and the empire can be paralleled—in all instances the "queer" other becomes antithetical whilst the female must be penetrated for the successful birth of democracy and freedom, the children of American insemination.

Notes

1   The imperial project as a masculine pursuit could also be applied to the other side of Harvey's capitalist imperialism which refers to "'the molecular processes of capital accumulation in space and time' (imperialism as a diffuse political-economic process in space and time which command over and use of capital takes primacy)" (2003, p. 25). It is clear that this imperial domination is entrenched in capitalist motives. However, for the purpose of my argument I will not be explicitly focusing on this aspect.

2   This of course is tied up with notions of racial and cultural superiority which will be touched on throughout my essay.

3   This process can also be seen to result in Islamophobia which is developed in the American metropolis and projected overseas in the movement of bodies—Islamophobia acts to build American identity and fuels the war overseas.

4   Homosexuality was seen as a symbol of degeneracy in colonial England. This defining of the "gay degenerate" also takes on narratives of racial and gendered "othering" which can be paralleled with my argument towards the "othering" of citizens in Afghanistan and Iraq (see Somerville, 1994).

5   Through a Derridean narrative of différancem—the lack of what British society considered masculine attributes pitted Indian men on the opposite side of the gendered binary, as effeminate.

6   There is an inherent tension between the heterosexual and homosocial nature of this space which can lead to contradiction. This will be outlined later in my essay.

7   Or exempt, this depends how you conceptualize women's "rights" when it comes to inclusion in violent institutions like the military. Also, Israel is the exception to this statement as Israeli women face a mandatory military service. With that said, they must only serve two years whilst their male counterparts must serve three.

8   We can also make note of the flight suits Bush was often seen wearing and the comical and public speculation that was made as to if President Bush had stuffed the crotch of these suits in an attempt to flaunt his undeniable masculinity.

9   "Cojones" means testicles in colloquial Spanish.

10 See   www.awec.info,   www.trustineducation.com, www.womenforafghanwomen.com,   www.hawca.org, www.cw4wafghan.ca, for but a few of the innumerable NGOs and IGOs dedicated to saving Afghan and Iraqi women and children.

11 The film only discusses heterosexual assault of men on women and barely mentions male sexual assault by men. This could be seen to further perpetuate the American military as a heterosexual space.

12 The start-date for this statistic is not clear.

13 Another point of consideration is the position in which these men, guilty of rape, are placed. While they are also here to emancipate Muslim women they are subjugating their female counterparts to the same oppression.

14 It is not my intention to conflate masculinity and violence in all instances, rather I would argue that the military is a violent and masculine institution—these two characteristics have a positive relationship with each influencing one another.

15 See Puar's *Queer Times, Terrorist Assemblages* (2007) and her discussion of American "*exceptionalism*"; a dualistic global conception of America's "queer identity". Wherein Firstly America is made to seem exceptional – in that it is accepting of queer identities (this could be exemplified in the repeal of the Don't Ask Don't Tell policy). Secondly America is seen as "exceptional" in that queer identities are portrayed as the exception or atypical.

References

Armanios, F., & Margesson, R. (2004). *Congressional Research Service Report Assistance to Afghan and Iraqi Women: Issues for Congress* (RS21865).
http://wikileaks.org/wiki/CRS-RS21865

Barklow, T. K.; Ziering, A.; & Dick, K. (Directors). (2012). *The Invisible War* [Motion picture]. USA: Chain Camera Pictures.

Beale, J. (2006). Diary: Rice's Mid-East Mission. *BBC News*, July 26.
http://news.bbc.co.uk/1/hi/world/middle_east/5205164.stm

Benatar, D. (2012). *The Second Sexism: Discrimination against Men and Boys*. Malden, MA: Wiley-Blackwell.

Benedict, H. (2007). The Private War of Women Soldiers. *Salon*, March 7. http://www.salon.com/2007/03/07/women_in_military/

Britton, D. M., & Williams, C. L. (1995). "Don't Ask, Don't Tell, Don't Pursue": Military Policy and the Construction of Heterosexual Masculinity. *Journal of Homosexuality*, 30(1), 1–21.

Connell, R. W. (1995). *Masculinities*. Berkeley, CA: University of California Press.

————. (2005). *Masculinities*, 2nd ed. Cambridge, UK: Polity Press.

Crary, D. (2012). Don't Ask Don't Tell: Furor Fades A Year After Military's Gay Ban Lifted. *Huffington Post*, June 16. http://www.huffingtonpost.com/2012/09/16/dont-ask-dont-tell-furor-subsides_n_1888454.html

Edelman, L. (1998). The Future Is Kid Stuff: Queer Theory, Disidentification, and the Death Drive. In D. E. Hall & A. Jagose (Eds.), *The Routledge Queer Studies Reader* (pp. 60–73). London, UK: Routledge.

Faiez, R., & Vogt, H. (2012). Taliban Poisoned School Girls, Say Afghanistan Officials. *Huffington Post*, June 6. http://www.huffingtonpost.com/2012/06/06/taliban-poison-school-girls-afghanistan_n_1573325.html

Filkins, D. (2009). Afghan Girls, Scarred by Acid, Defy Terror, Embracing School. *The New York Times*, January 13. http://www.nytimes.com/2009/01/14/world/asia/14kandahar.html

Hanifi, M. J. (2009). Afghanistan's Little Girls on the Front Line, Part 2. *Zero Anthropology*, August 17. http://zeroanthropology.net/2009/08/17/afghanistans-little-girls-on-the-front-line-part-2/

Harvey, D. (2003). *The New Imperialism*. Oxford: Oxford University Press.

Krishnaswamy, R. (1998). *Effeminism: The Economy of Colonial Desire*. Ann Arbor: University of Michigan Press.

Major, E. (2012). *Madam Britannia: Women, Church, and Nation, 1712–1812*. Oxford, UK: Oxford University Press.

McClintock, A. (2013). Paranoid Empire, Imperial Ghosting, and Gender Violence. *Rethinking Race and Sexuality: Feminist Conversations, Contestations, and Coalitions*. Lecture conducted from Concordia University, Montreal, QC, April.

Mulvey, L. (1990). Visual Pleasure and Narrative Cinema. In P. Erens (Ed.), *Issues in Feminist Film Criticism* (pp. 57–68). Bloomington: Indiana University Press. (Original work published 1973).

Nesiah, V. (2012). Feminism as Counterterroism? *The Wrong King of Green*, August 16. http://wrongkindofgreen.org/2012/08/16/feminism-as-counterterrorism/

Palmer, J. (2009). Taliban Kill Afghan Students, Burn Schools. *The Washington Times*, May 28. http://www.washingtontimes.com/news/2009/may/28/taliban-takes-battle-to-schools/

Puar, J. K. (2005). Queer Times, Queer Assemblages. *Social Text*, 23(3–4), 121–139.

———— . (2007). *Terrorist Assemblages: Homonationalism in Queer Times*. Durham, NC: Duke University Press.

Said, E. W. (1979). *Orientalism*. New York: Vintage Books.

Segal, L. (2008). Gender, War and Militarism: Making and Questioning the Links. *Feminist Review*, 88, 21–35.

Somerville, S. (1994). Scientific Racism and the Emergence of the Homosexual Body. *Journal of the History of Sexuality*, 5(2), 243–266.

Stanton, J. (2011). U.S. Army Female Engagement Teams Expand: King Xerxes' Queen Esther Cited. *Zero Anthropology*, January 4. http://zeroanthropology.net/2011/01/04/u-s-army-female-engagement-teams-expand-king-xerxes%E2%80%99-queen-esther-cited/

Webster, W. (1998). *Imagining Home: Gender, "Race," and National Identity, 1945–64*. London, UK: UCL Press.

Woodman, B. J. (2003). A Hollywood War of Wills: Cinematic Representation of Vietnamese Super-Soldiers and America's Defeat in the War. *Journal of Film and Video*, 55(2/3), 44–58.

Woodward, B. (2004). *Plan of Attack*. New York, NY: Simon & Schuster.

Zada, S., & Santana, R. (2012). Taliban Gunmen Shoot 14-Year-Old Girl Activist. *Associated Press*, October 9. http://bigstory.ap.org/article/pakistan-probes-barter-7-girls-settle-feud

CHAPTER THREE

America's Own Backyard: Hurricane Katrina and Military Intervention

Angela Noel

On August 29, 2005, Hurricane Katrina hit the Mississippi Gulf Coast, striking one of the most vulnerable communities in the U.S. Ranked as the 10th most segregated city in the U.S., New Orleans continues to remain the victim of a neoliberal agenda of exploitation (Brym, 2008). With poverty rates remaining strikingly high, especially in the most exposed regions, the crescent city experienced what was to be America's largest natural disaster. While the hurricane was a natural disaster, the flooding of New Orleans was a preventable and predictable event. So how is it that the U.S, with its powerful military force and "noble" interventions was unable to aid one of their own most historically and culturally rich communities? Is humanitarian intervention solely about getting involved in other nation-states?

New Orleans has flourished throughout a plethora of hardships, resilient, representative of civil rights history, and heavy with a legacy of struggles for freedom and equality with which the U.S. identifies. New Orleans is a city that embraces tragedy and celebrates victory through its multi-cultural Carnival. It is also home to an outstanding amount of musical history. Louis Armstrong, Fats Domino, Dr. John, Irma Hayes and a never-ending list of musicians who have shaped global musical history, arisen from New Orleans' Creole melting pot. New Orleans was home even to political rebels such as Benito Juarez, a Zapotec lawyer who lived in New Orleans from 1853 to 1855 as a cigar maker, before eventually becoming President of Mexico (Lipsitz, 2006, p. 459). The citizens of New Orleans continue to celebrate with friendly attitudes and open arms, but underneath lies a history of adversity.

New Orleans: A Historical Canvas

By 1840, New Orleans was the fourth most populous city in the U.S. and in the 1920s it became the city of jazz (Brym, 2008, p. 55). Renowned for its French architecture and mystical swamps, many films such as *Interview with the Vampire* have been shot in New Orleans. However, the city is dangerously situated. Much of New Orleans rests below sea level—sometimes by as much as 2.5 metres (Brym, 2008, p. 55). On top of that, approximately 1.5 metres of rain falls on New Orleans every year, more than twice that of Toronto (Brym, 2008, p. 56), and even ocean water often washes up into New Orleans.

The French settled in 1718 as a hub of the North American interior in order to control trade, to bridge French settlements, and to create a barrier against British settlers. French Canadian and German colonists began to arrive along with West African slaves joining French and First Nations people in an early multi-cultural melting pot. Intermarriage was not as frowned upon at this time and created the distinct ethnic group referred to as Louisiana Creole. When war arose in the mid-1800s between Britain and France, Spain took control for 38 years until finally the French sold Louisiana to the U.S. for $15 million in what is called the Louisiana purchase. Now that it had become official American territory, many white settlers moved to New Orleans and it became the country's largest port between 1810 and 1860 (Brym, 2008, p. 58).

Racial tensions were lulled by French ideals of equality that allowed freed slaves successful job opportunities in trades and on docks. These tensions resurged as white Americans took over the jobs in trades and on docks previously held by African Americans, creating a racialized class conflict that caused some freed slaves to leave for Haiti. Racism grew as Louisiana fought to protect slavery during the civil war and segregation laws came into effect from 1861–1865. A series of laws, such as Jim Crow, kept white and black people apart, whether on trains, at dances, sports teams, neighbourhoods and even banned cohabitation (Brym, 2008, p. 61).

In the late 1920s, as levee construction began and created isolated real estate for white Americans, the suburbs became the most popular neighbourhood for white residents. This made African Americans become the majority of the population of New Orleans, particularly the most vulnerable regions such as the neighbourhood most affected by Hurricane Katrina, the Lower Ninth Ward. Up until the storm, New Orleans was 68% African American, 25% non-Hispanic white and the poverty rate for African Americans was 35%, which is 7.5% higher than that of the national average for African Americans (Brym, 2008; 61). Education and healthcare were neglected. The New Orleans Police Department (NOPD) was notoriously corrupt and racist. New Orleans was slowly becoming a neoliberal state, leaving the black population incredibly vulnerable.

Preparing New Orleans for Disaster

To say that a massive hurricane in the gulf coast region was a common prediction is an understatement. Even the Federal Emergency Management Agency (FEMA) had a report issued in 2001 stating that the chances of "a hurricane striking New Orleans was one of the three most likely disasters to hit the United States" (Brym, 2008, p. 54). This apparently was not enough for the U.S. or Louisiana to properly prepare for such a catastrophe. Two factors played large parts in this, according to Robert J. Brym: 1) the disappearance of coastal wetlands; and, 2) the inadequacy of the levees. The marshes and barrier islands of the wetlands protect New Orleans: for every 3.2 km of wetland, the storm surge reduces by 15 cm. Before the levees were built, silt helped to prevent the sinking of Gulf wetlands. Since the levees were built, they have diverted silt into the Gulf, creating a rapid dissipation of the wetlands. The diminished wetlands, which acted as a buffer, meant that warm seawater could come closer to New Orleans, and the warm vapour needed to sustain a hurricane would thus at least sustain its strength as it approached the city (Brym, 2008, p. 61). The inadequacy of the levees, built in 1927, is another hurricane risk, as the walls surrounding Lake Pontchartrain had not been reinforced since Hurricane Betsy, which killed more than 70 people in 1965. The U.S. Army Corps of Engineers had been assigned to build the walls to withstand a category 3 storm, but after 40 years they were in desperate need of upgrading. Hurricane Katrina was, in fact, a category 3 storm. However, due to neglect half the levees were damaged and New Orleans, always at risk of a potential category 5 hurricane, stood at less readiness than needed to meet a category 3 hurricane (Brym, 2008, p. 62).

In 2003, the George W. Bush administration allowed unrestricted development of the wetlands, and refused to pay $14 billion to restore the wetlands and barrier islands. This amount would have equalled only six weeks at war in Iraq (Brym, 2008, p. 63).

The Militarization of New Orleans

"Every gun that is made, every warship launched, every rocket fired, signifies in the final sense a theft from those who hunger and are not fed, those who are cold and are not clothed." – Dwight D. Eisenhower

Governor of Louisiana Kathleen Blanco made an official announcement three days before the storm, declaring a state of emergency, after the hurricane advisory board had made it clear that this storm was going to be a major hurricane by the time it hit Louisiana (Farmer, 2011, pp. 16–17). This was a storm that FEMA should have been well prepared for as they had run a disaster simulation exercise, "Hurricane Pam," in 2004 which revealed New Orleans's extreme susceptibility. Despite these warnings, Mayor Ray Nagin had only issued a mandatory evacuation one day prior to the storm on August 27 and the Louisiana National Guard had issued a request for 700 buses from FEMA, but only provided 100 and because many residents of New Orleans could not afford to leave, 30,000 people were stranded at the Superdome where they were promised food and shelter. FEMA, however, did not expect this amount of people and there was a severe lack of water, medical aid and food (Farmer, 2011, p. 17).

On August 28, Hurricane Katrina had become a category 4 storm. At that point, mainstream media coverage jumped from reporting the disaster to instead spreading a sense of panic about looters, with reports claiming that residents were being shot, raped, that looting had broken out and gangs roamed the streets, and that law enforcement agents and rescue helicopters were being shot at. The reality was that only eight gunshot victims were reported during the hurricane in total, two of which were suicides (Farmer, 2011, p. 18). There was also no tangible evidence of any shooting towards helicopters, but if there was it is very possible that the alleged shooters were simply attempting to draw attention towards themselves and seek help. Looters were for the most part probably just people lost and in search for food and water which is not a shocking or sinister motive. Essentially the news media fostered mass hysteria, which prevented New Orleans from receiving life-saving help. This is not an uncommon phenomenon: disaster research has reported that panic is often created during disasters to alarm the public, when in reality crime is not a higher risk following disasters in the U.S. The creation of a sense of panic provided the U.S. government with justification for military involvement, as several thousand fully armed National Guard troops enforced a 6:00pm curfew for everyone regardless of whether they were in search of their friends and family. Military checkpoints were put in place as New Orleans became an occupied territory and the police were even granted the right to shoot looters who posed no immediate threat to the public. Federal response to Hurricane Katrina was less about the protection of American citizens, and about enforcing discipline and protecting private property. More focus was placed on preventing crime than rescuing victims.

There was also an unquestionable element of racism as black residents were profiled in newspapers as "looters" and white citizens were the first to receive aid (Brym, 2008, p. 73) and often Katrina victims were labelled as "refugees" of the storm. Alongside the National Guard, private military companies (PMCs) and even foreign troops, namely Blackwater and the Israeli Defence Forces respectively, were hired to assist in "crime prevention" in New Orleans and to guard private property (Farmer, 2011, p. 23). Aid reports during the storm certainly focused on surveillance and crime prevention, but not as much was mentioned with respect to medical aid or search and rescue. Administrative failures arose due to a lack of planning between federal, local and state governments with non-profits concerning disaster tactics.

Hurricane Katrina was the first major hurricane to hit the U.S. while covered by live television. In the process, Americans who were previously invisible to the media eye, were exposed: namely, masses of poor and desperate African American victims. Editors of the *Kenya Daily* were in disbelief that the coverage they were viewing was of the U.S., with such a disproportionate amount of black refugees (Eikenberry, Arroyave, & Cooper, 2007, p. 164).

Figure 3.1: Iwo Jima in New Orleans

The USS Iwo Jima (LHD 7) arrives outside the French Quarter of New Orleans to serve as a floating launch pad for amphibious and air operations in the aftermath of Hurricane Katrina. (U.S. Air National Guard Photo by TSgt Paul Gorman, public domain).

The military certainly had other duties it could have performed alongside crime prevention. Aircraft could have been deployed to search for on-going damage and water pockets surrounding the city. All in all, the treatment of New Orleans was that of a security mission abroad, not one about saving their own citizens. A valid question pertains to the source of the alleged "threat" to public safety, given that it was five officers of the very police department of New Orleans that were found guilty of the shooting that occurred on the Danziger Bridge in the days after Hurricane Katrina, leaving two innocent civilians dead and four others seriously wounded (U.S. Department of Justice [DOJ], 2012).

There are many criticisms of the role of government in dealing with the devastating hurricane, from the mishandling of Mayor Ray Nagin, to the levee neglect, to President Bush's preoccupation with the war on Iraq. A strong criticism of the post-Katrina treatment of New Orleans stems from a questionable implementation of the military in disaster control. The *Posse Comitatus Act* (1878) was originally created to restrict the federal government from applying the use of the military in law enforcement matters. However, in 1981 an amendment was made allowing the military to intervene in cases of civil unrest or disasters (Tkacz, 2006, p. 309). Prior to 1981, there were many historical exceptions to the Act, including the 1981 amendment at the Wounded Knee protests where local, state and federal law enforcement engaged in a 71-day confrontation between the American Indian Movement (AIM) on the Sioux Nation that many First Nations people considered to be an unlawful violation and was later debated in courts (Tkacz, 2006, p. 310).

Many factors have led to the militarization of aid in the U.S., and with widespread fear of terrorism, its presence has only increased. Meanwhile, federal power has steadily risen in the U.S. as far back as the Federal Civil Defence Act in 1950 and the Stafford Act (originally the Disaster Relief Act created in 1974) which allowed the federal government to take direct action in the event of natural disasters—the use of the military was to be an exception, to be employed solely in aid of civil authorities. In 1979, the Federal Emergency Management Agency (FEMA) took over as the primary disaster handling agency due to the concern of the federal government's inability to coordinate disasters (Farmer, 2011, pp. 11–12). An earlier shift from civil defense to preparedness for natural disasters, was reversed after 9/11. By 2003, FEMA became a formal part of the Department of Homeland Security (DHS)

(Farmer, 2011, p. 13). Inclusion within Homeland Security had consequences, as Farmer (2011, p. 13) explains,

> "The main focus of the DHS since its creation has been national security and terrorism, so natural disaster response preparedness efforts and mitigation plans were superseded by counter terrorism as the new homeland security focused organization developed plans based on terrorist disasters".

Moreover, many of the early heads of FEMA themselves had military experience and had spent almost $3 billion on disaster preparedness in the event of nuclear war between 1982 and 1991 (Farmer, 2011, p. 12). Having said that, five of the eight top officials at FEMA had *no* disaster experience, including its head at the time of Hurricane Katrina, Michael Brown, but were instead loyal appointees of President Bush (Brym, 2008, p. 70).

The focus of the DHS was almost purely on managing and preventing acts of terrorism, even releasing a document titled "How Terrorists Might Exploit a Hurricane" in 2004, an unlikely event but leading to the eventual security checks in New Orleans shelters during the storm (Farmer, 2011, p. 14). In the creation of the National Response Plan (2004), a "counter-terrorism think tank," the Rand Corporation, was contracted to draft the plan, rather than FEMA (Farmer, 2011, p. 15). Insufficient attention was paid to disaster management in the creation of the National Response Plan due to an increased focus in terrorism post-9/11. References are still being made to 9/11 when the White House speaks of Hurricane Katrina, as if New Orleans was not part of their own country, bur rather on the military's radar as the target of another act of terrorism.

Historically, the military has been involved in disaster relief, but Hurricane Katrina provides us with an entirely new example of just how reliant the U.S. state has become on the military as its national bodyguard. On the other hand, as Farmer (2011, p. 28) argues, while the concern for complete control and avoidance of risk is widespread, the reigning neoliberal doctrine posits that citizens must also take action in safeguarding their own wellbeing when disasters strike. Thus a massive network of military and intelligence agencies can coexist with instructions to citizens to purchase duct tape and plastic sheets to guard against chemical attacks. As security is increasingly privatized, citizens are expected to prepare for such crises themselves while the government assumes less responsibility to manage such unpredictable events. The residents of New Orleans are a key example of a population vulnerable due to the effects of neo-liberalism. With poverty rates rising and institutional racism, poor and black citizens are left to the margins and become increasingly unprepared and at great risk to lose what little they have worked very hard to gain.

The neglect of New Orleans, when it was common knowledge that the city was at severe risk in the event of a major hurricane, effectively meant that risk was manufactured (Farmer, 2011, p. 30). By means of "othering" the poor, often black citizens of a high-crime city, a moral panic takes place when disaster strikes. Without sufficient education from the federal government to prepare for such a risk, Americans are fearful of the unknown consequences. Being kept in the dark and then exposed to such a tragedy creates mass shock, at the same time creating the perfect opportunity for a fear-mongering government to take advantage of citizens by offering military assistance. This is when even the police department maintains a military presence, with inhumane and unconstitutional shoot to kill orders. This disaster was indeed a manufactured risk and the crime risk was manufactured to use crime as scapegoat by the Bush administration as the foremost cause for aid and intervention.

The Voluntary Failure and the Non-Profit Industrial Complex

"'Emergencies' have always been the pretext on which the safeguards of individual liberty have been eroded." – Freidrich August von Hayek

"The substantial response by international actors to Katrina may underscore that the United States has much to learn about disaster preparedness, management, and recovery from other nations." (Eikenberry, Arroyave, & Cooper, 2007, p. 167)

Despite President Bush's praise of FEMA, the fact that the U.S. severely failed in dealing with disaster relief in New Orleans is considered to be the "biggest administrative failure in U.S. history" (Eikenberry, Arroyave, & Cooper, 2007, p. 160). What distinguishes Hurricane Katrina from many natural disasters is that it was a historical event in which global aid towards the U.S. was higher than ever, including NGOs and international non-governmental organizations (INGOs). Unprecedented offers of aid were flowing in from around the world, including a significant amount of aid from developing countries such as Venezuela and Cuba, with Fidel Castro graciously offering 1,586 doctors carrying approximately 27 pounds of medicine each—and he received "absolutely no response" (Newman, 2005).

When approximately $3.3 billion in private donations are raised and nearly every charitable organization in the U.S. and beyond are contributing to alleviate the disaster of a developed country, an imperial superpower at that, it is either a very telling sign of how far that power has fallen or a sign of how it treats its own citizens. Among the INGOs present were: the International Medical Corps (IMC) who were valuable due to their expertise in disaster settings; the International Rescue Committee (IRC) who normally focus on victims of war and persecution; the American Refugee Committee (ARC) who provided water, sanitation, shelter and healthcare to FEMA; as well as the Red Cross and UNICEF which for the first time in 55 years used its "Trick-or-Treat for Unicef" program to raise funds for American children (Eikenberry, Arroyave, & Cooper, 2007, p. 161).

Hurricane Katrina provided yet another excuse for the justification of military force as the military was viewed as the only body capable of "controlling" such a situation when, in the end, the disaster's effects were produced by a lack of emergency preparedness and a mass mediated hysteria about crime. Numerous INGOs, according to Eikenberry, Arroyave, and Cooper, perceived the response to Hurricane Katrina as being in stark contrast to the response to 9/11. In the chaos surrounding the flooding, it appeared as if there was no system at all in place to deal with disasters and in particular with the distribution of aid. There was a common perception that the U.S. would have more infrastructures in place and that relief work would be much less of an effort than in developing countries. Organizations were confused because there appeared to be no standards in place (Eikenberry, Arroyave, & Cooper, 2007, p. 165), and often INGOs received late responses or none at all from governmental agencies. In a telephone interview, an INGO staff member exclaimed, "nobody could get through to anybody to tell them they were needed to come" (Eikenberry, Arroyave, & Cooper, 2007, p. 165), with confusion taking place at all levels as local officials sought to deliver resources but were met with a lack of clarity as to how they were expected to be provided. Hurricane Katrina is thus considered to be what some call a *voluntary* failure: "voluntary failure in terms of philanthropic insufficiency, particularism, paternalism and amateurism" (Eikenberry, Arroyave, & Cooper, 2007, p. 166).

The issues of poverty, dependency, and privatized relief are also critical. Citizens who ordinarily are dependent for support from government may find themselves submitting to the paternalism of large NGOs and INGOs, which introduces another problem. The problem here is that goals of self-determination and sustainability in mutual aid cannot be achieved by short, ad hoc solutions managed by external interests. Cindi Katz describes the situation post-Katrina as the "non-profit industrial complex" (Katz, 2008, p. 25) after the U.S. government essentially vacated the disaster relief scene, opening it to non-governmental bodies. The inherent coloniality of governing disenfranchised citizens who are considered unable to govern themselves is especially problematic for people in the U.S. South. This pertains to the rise of what some call the "non-profit industrial complex," where "priorities and modes of practice are set by donors and not those in need, and 'accountability' is a one-way street determined by the funders" (Katz, 2008, p. 25). In the case of Hurricane Katrina, organizations such as The Red Cross, Salvation Army, United Way and the Bush Clinton Katrina fund absorbed the majority of donations, "with the Red Cross outstripping the others by a long shot, despite their poor track record on getting funds where most needed, their inefficiency, and their lack of accountability—the very things to which they hold local organizations strictly answerable," leading many to refer to such trends as the "Halliburtonization" of the non-profit sector (Katz, 2008, p. 25). The most powerful non-profit groups thus often became large businesses that built their strength from such disasters.

NGOs have become a staple in U.S. governance. Not only are they a paramount force in disaster relief in the U.S., but they serve as a major pillar of the economy as well:

"According to the National Center for Charitable Statistics (NCCS), the sector accounts for a significant share of employment (7% in 2009); representing 9% of the economy's wages and salaries....The sector also contributed US$779 billion in expenditures—an estimated 5.4% of the nation's gross domestic product (GDP) in 2010....As of November 2011, the Internal Revenue Service (IRS) reported a total of 1.58 million registered nonprofits (including private foundations). Of these, the 1.16 million nonprofits filing 990 forms with the IRS generated a total of US$1.94 trillion in revenue and US$6.36 trillion in total assets....The growth rate was 25%

between 2001 and 2011, surpassing that of the private and public sectors". (Chikoto, Sadiq, & Fordyce, 2013, p. 394)

Paternalism and the New Imperialism

In the aftermath of the storm the U.S. racial divide seems to have grown, as systemic racism prevails. George Bush's Secretary of Housing and Urban Development Alphonso Jackson could not have been clearer when he stated, "New Orleans is not going to be as black as it was for a long time, if ever again" (Lipsitz, 2006, p. 453). Now more than ever, New Orleans' poor and black residents bear the brunt of neoliberal agendas. Facing severe housing discrimination due to the refusal to enforce fair housing laws, living in unsafe homes and lacking transportation to exit the city whilst businesses earned tax breaks, the citizens of New Orleans have not been left with much (Lipsitz, 2006, p. 452). Lack of access to proper medical care and exposure to toxic chemicals in FEMA trailers (Verderber, 2008) left some of the most vulnerable citizens of the U.S. in squalid conditions—with or without help from NGOs. Though a reported $7 billion has been spent on the levees post-Katrina, reports suggest that once again, New Orleans remains at risk (Katz, 2008).

Some would argue that what New Orleans experienced is part of a larger syndrome of long-term U.S. imperialism. As Katz put it, "the hostile privatism, speculative instrumentalism, and counter-subversive carceralism that characterized the Bush Administration's response to the war in Iraq and to Hurricane Katrina have deep roots in contemporary American culture" (Katz, 2008, p. 29). This is to say that there is a connection between the imperialist paternalism evoked during the initial Iraq invasion and the disregard of New Orleans by FEMA, George Bush and the Department of Homeland Security. This connection represents the "othering" of both national and international minorities by the U.S., an othering process that takes on paternalist expressions. Imperial America arguably expresses a paternalist mentality towards its own citizens and citizens of the world. However, that paternalism is not "equal," in the sense that it is still selective along racial lines. During Hurricane Katrina, there were several examples of this selectivity as white citizens were asked to evacuate first and received more treatment than black residents of New Orleans (Brym, 2008, p. 76).

U.S. citizens have also begun to lose their rights in the name of privatization, security and militarization. As David Harvey put it, "empire abroad entails tyranny at home....Military activity abroad requires military-like discipline at home" (Harvey, 2005, p. 193). If there were any way of defining the military's role in Hurricane Katrina, it would be *disciplinary*:

> "They were all about detention, as if it were Iraq, like we were foreigners and they were fighting a war. They implemented war-like conditions. They treated us worse than prisoners of war. Even prisoners of war have rights under the Geneva convention". (Leah Hodges, quoted in Brym, 2008, p. 78)

References

Brym, R. J. (2008). *Sociology As a Life Or Death Issue*. Belmont, CA: Wadsworth.

Chikoto, G. L.; Sadiq, A.-A.; & Fordyce, E. (2013). Disaster Mitigation and Preparedness: Comparison of Nonprofit, Public, and Private Organizations. *Nonprofit and Voluntary Sector Quarterly*, 42(2), 391–410.

Eikenberry, A. M.; Arroyave, V.; & Cooper, T. (2007). Administrative Failure and the International NGO Response to Hurricane Katrina. *Public Administration Review*, 67, 160–170.

Farmer, A. K. (2011). A Call to Arms: The Militarization of Natural Disasters in the United States. *Online Theses and Dissertations*, Paper 34.
http://encompass.eku.edu/etd/34

Harvey, D. (2005). *The New Imperialism*. New York, NY: Oxford University Press.

Katz, C. (2008). Bad Elements: Katrina and the Scoured Landscape of Social Reproduction. *Gender, Place & Culture*, 15(1), 15–29.

Lipsitz, G. (2006). Learning from New Orleans: The Social Warrant of Hostile Privatism and Competitive Consumer Citizenship. *Cultural Anthropology*, 21(3), 451–468.

Newman, L. (2005). Castro: U.S. Hasn't Responded to Katrina Offer. *CNN*, September 5.
http://edition.cnn.com/2005/WORLD/americas/09/05/katrina.cuba/

Tkacz, S. R. (2006). In Katrina's Wake: Rethinking the Military's Role in Domestic Emergencies. *William and Mary Bill of Rights Journal*, 15(1), 301–334.

U.S. Department of Justice (DOJ). (2012). Five New Orleans Police Officers Sentenced on Civil Rights and Obstruction of Justice Violations in the Danziger Bridge Shooting Case. Washington, DC: Department of Justice, Office of Public Affairs.

http://www.justice.gov/opa/pr/2012/April/12-crt-430.html

Verderber, S. (2008). Emergency housing in the aftermath of Hurricane Katrina: an assessment of the FEMA travel trailer program. Journal of Housing and the Built Environment, 23(4), 367–381.

CHAPTER FOUR

The Prying Eye and the Iron Fist: State Surveillance and Police Militarization

Kyle McLoughlin

O n the morning of September 4, 2008, police tactical teams formed from members of the Ramsay County Sheriff's Department carried out a no-knock raid on several properties in St. Paul, Minnesota. Clad in body armour and armed with semi-automatic assault rifles the officers' actions were the culmination of months of investigations conducted by a diverse team of law enforcement agencies and their partners in the private sector. Their targets were a broad coalition of political activists and organizers that included peace activists, anarchists, and anti-authoritarians from across the U.S. who had converged on the city of Saint Paul to protest the Republican National Convention. The Republican National Convention Welcoming Committee (RNC-WC), perhaps the largest coalition of radicals preparing for the convention, was the subject of a sophisticated and heavily militarized system of social control. State security agencies, revolutionized by the demands of the War on Terror, identified the RNC-WC as one of the most significant threats to the proceedings of the convention because of a conflation of non-normative or radical political opposition with that of terrorist activity. Political behaviour outside of those practices acceptable to authority—such as permitted marches or pressuring one's representative to effect legislative change—is identified and prosecuted as a threat to national security. This was in an effort to isolate dissidence and crush a resistance that refused to have its political expression institutionalized;

to alienate and anathematize the RNC-WC behind the mythical shroud of the War on Terror. These domestic campaigns are, unsurprisingly given the rhetoric of the war metaphor, waged like the missions abroad using an extensive network of intelligence operatives to gather information on potential threats, whether real or imagined, which are in turn eliminated by the aggressive tactics of a police force equipped for a domestic insurgency.

Recent developments among state, local, and federal law enforcement agencies have indicated a methodological and practical shift towards militarist ideology in their enforcement of social control. These developments are nothing new as Graeber (2013) writes that there is a long history of police violence meted out towards campaigns for social justice, ranging from the Red Scare's suppression of growing resistance among labour to a campaign of murder against radicals involved in the respective Red and Black power movements. The attacks on the World Trade centre on September 11, 2001, catalyzed the development of a militarized security state in two respects. First, there has been a systematic transfer of military equipment including assault rifles, armoured personnel carriers, and tactical gear to civilian law enforcement agencies. These resources come from direct material transfers from the Department of Defense (DoD) which provides military surplus gear at little to no cost as well as financial grants provided by the Department of Homeland Security (DHS) used to bolster local agencies under the banner of national security. Similar transfers have taken place historically, however language within the *Posse Comitatus Act* and the *Insurrection Act* had effectively created a barrier to the DoD from taking a more active role in domestic policing (Fisher, 2010).

Second is the expansion of the state surveillance and intelligence gathering apparatus. Just as with material support to security agencies, policies that regulate domestic surveillance have been amended over time to expand the capabilities of the security state to gather and share information. The formation of the Department of Homeland Security in 2002 consolidated a legislative and administrative framework under which numerous domestic intelligence gathering agencies could operate with expanded power. The archetype of this relationship is manifested in the intelligence fusion centres which are information processing hubs established by state and local law enforcement, funded primarily by the Department of Homeland Security, and staffed by intelligence analysts from agencies including the Central Intelligence Agency and the Federal Bureau of Investigation. Fusion centres aggregate data received from state, local law, and federal enforcement agencies, the Department of Defense, as well as private corporations. Content gathered includes suspicious activity reports created by law enforcement, passive or soft data generated by internet and cell phone use, as well as information gathered through proactive surveillance operations. Through fusion centres, analysts create threat profiles based on data trends and surveillance reports. This information is then passed on to investigatory and enforcement elements for follow-up and execute pre-emptive action against supposed threats to national security.

The two elements of the state security apparatus listed above form a powerful synergy. Intelligence fusion centres form threat profiles using privileged access to government and private information databases which, in conjunction with information gathered through expanded legislative powers, are used to identify targets. This target acquisition is then followed by investigation and arrest carried out by a more militarized police force than ever before. This relationship can be seen in the tactics of the War on Drugs where military radar and surveillance planes provide intelligence for joint anti-drug task forces which then execute raids utilizing paramilitary policing units equipped with weaponry and gear provided, in part, by the Department of Defense (Fisher, 2010).

Another more insidious use of this escalated security relationship is in the continued suppression of political dissent. Such an operation took place in 2008 during which the domestic surveillance apparatus opened investigations into the RNC-WC. The conclusions of this investigation resulted in pre-emptive raids conducted by a militarized police force and court charges of conspiracy related to "terrorism". By using the security apparatus in such a way, the U.S. wages a domestic war to silence political dissent, suppress opposition and ensure that a culture of fear exists among any who would associate themselves with unconventional ideals.

Boots on the Ground:
Militarized Law Enforcement and PPUs

In form and in function all police agencies are militarized to varying degrees as police have access to the more or less legitimized use of violence in the maintenance of social control. This coercive authority is similar to that of the military in the sense that both rely on the legitimization of their violence to ensure maximum efficacy in their respective social roles. The divergence is in form and function (Kraska, 2007). Police forces, while able to employ physical coercive force, are intended in spirit to use the least amount of violence possible in the maintenance of peace and internal security, bound by regulation and accountable to civil society (Brown, 2011; Kraska, 2007). The military is intended to execute the external will of the state and has free reign to employ violence against its designated targets; there are boundaries, however they are far beyond the traditional limits of civilian police agencies. Blurring the two functions of each body is indicative of the state's militarist ideology. Militarist doctrine emphasizes using overwhelming, violent force as an accepted and effective solution to problems; the implementation of this ideology is the process of militarization (Kraska, 2007). The militarization of the police occurs when these two bodies, civil security and external security begin to converge. As the police begin to adopt the ideological and material assets of the state's armed forces, boundaries regulating their respective functions begin to collapse. The outcome of this process is the fusion of the soldier and civilian peacekeeper which further develops the militarist mindset of viewing crime as a threat to national security and alleged law breakers as enemy combatants: both to be executed as such (Kraska, 2007). The expression of national security frames state militarist actions as self-defence against enemy attack providing both justification and legitimization for preemptive action and overwhelming force against targets.

The rhetoric coming from law enforcement and respective political interests is one of waging a war on social problems (Hill & Beger, 2009). Kraska and Kappeler (1997) illustrate how the war metaphor stresses the use of coercive force as the most appropriate means of solving turmoil; threats to order are seen as enemies to be pacified. The coercive force inherent to policing is further escalated in the expansion of paramilitary policing units (PPUs), commonly referred to as SWAT teams. In past decades, police agencies perceived a need for specialized tactical teams, such as the PPUs, to respond to high risk situations such as mass shootings and hostage rescue raids; however, they are increasingly utilized in everyday police work (Kraska & Kappeler, 1997). Paramilitary policing units conceptually developed amid a period of social unrest throughout the late 1960s in the U.S. The contemporary SWAT team model formed in Los Angeles and became a permanent, full-time position within the city's police department by 1971 (Fisher, 2010). Kraska and Kappeler's study on the growth of militarized police forces show that law enforcement departments across the country followed Los Angeles and formed their own PPUs. By 1995, 89% of the 548 departments surveyed had formed paramilitary police units (Kraska & Kappeler, 1997, p. 6). These developments were not reserved solely for major metropolitan areas, reportedly 69% of smaller departments, serving jurisdictions between 25,000 and 50,000 people with less than 150 officers, had established a paramilitary unit by the time of their study.

While no national standardization process yet exists, generally speaking paramilitary police units are small, tactical teams that operate as a cohesive squad. Their form is modelled after military special operations units which in turn reinforces notions of the PPUs' elite nature in comparison to other law enforcement. PPUs' use of non-standard camouflage or all black uniforms further emphasizes their distinctness from everyday police units, further reinforcing a warrior mentality and detracting from spirit of police work. Kraska notes from his ethnographic work among American SWAT teams that paramilitary police culture is "characterized by a distinct techno-warrior garb, heavy weaponry, sophisticated technology, hyper masculinity, and dangerous function" (2007, p. 6), all traits consistent with militarist ideology that further distinguishes these units from everyday police despite the escalation in the use of paramilitary forces in everyday affairs.

Many PPUs have benefited from the vast transfer of equipment from the federal Department of Defense to local law enforcement agencies. Programs such as the Law Enforcement Support Office have enabled police agencies to access billions of dollars worth of military surplus at little to no cost (Fisher, 2010; Kraska, 2007). Formed in 1997 as part of the National Defense Authorization Act, the LESO continued a process begun in the early 1980s by the *Military Cooperation with Civilian Law Enforcement Act* to transfer excess military hardware to civilian agencies. After the formation of the Department of Homeland Security in 2002 state and local police agencies received additional windfall of funding through the *Urban Area Security Initiative (UASI)* to upgrade their training and equipment to better pursue the needs of the new War on Terrorism (Brown, 2011). These programs have facilitated the acquisition of weaponry and equipment such as assault rifles, grenade launchers, and armoured personnel carriers for both paramilitary units and everyday officers. An enquiry initiated by

Senator Tom Coburn into where DHS funding was being used showed that police departments have purchased so many armoured transports using the UASI grant that Lenco Armoured Vehicles, manufacturer of the popular BearCat APC, has started offering, free of charge, grant template materials and an eight-page guide to acquiring DHS funding (Coburn, 2012). Senator Coburn's report also highlights the proclivity of armoured fighting vehicles procured through DHS grants in areas of low Crime. Fargo, North Dakota a city with fewer than two homicides per year since 2005, purchased an armoured truck with rotating gun turrets using UASI money, as did Burbank, California, whose police department purchased a BearCat to replace an older APC that they had never deployed (Coburn, 2012). Furthermore, police departments have shown interest in procuring unmanned aerial vehicles, referred to as drones, using DHS grants. The lack of clarity in legislation regulating the domestic use of drones as well as the recent introduction of the technology so far has limited grant applications for purchasing unmanned aerial vehicles using federal money to just a handful of cities. The Miami-Dade Police Department purchased two drones in 2009 using grants from the Justice Department; a drone was purchased by the Arlington, Texas police department in 2011 for use during the Super Bowl after which the department searched for funding to continue its use; and, in 2011 the Seattle Police Department procured a USAI grant to purchase a drone (Coburn, 2012). As in the case of APCs, manufacturers of drones, such as Vanguard Defense Industries, readily supply law enforcement agencies with aid in writing federal grant applications.

Equipped to a level reminiscent of front line combat troops paramilitary police units are increasingly used for routine, comparatively low-risk police work. Kraska notes that between 1980 and 2000 there was more than a 1,400% increase in the total number of paramilitary police deployments for a contemporary approximation of 45,000 deployments per year in the departments surveyed (2007, p. 6). Of these deployments, the vast majority were not in response to high-risk situations; rather, 80% of SWAT deployments were for proactive drug raids searching private residences for contraband. Furthermore, many police departments utilize PPUs for routine patrol work, exemplified by one department's approach:

"We're into saturation patrols in hot spots. We do a lot of our work with the SWAT unit because we have bigger guns. We send out two, two-to-four-men cars, we look for minor violations and do jump-outs, either on people on the street or automobiles. After we jump-out the second car provides periphery cover with an ostentatious display of weaponry. We're sending a clear message: if the shootings don't stop, we'll shoot someone". (Quoted in Kraska & Kappeler, 1997, p. 10)

The continued rise of paramilitary police units in conjunction with militarization of everyday law enforcement personnel fit within the war metaphor articulated by state security agencies: soldiers require the best tools for the job and the federal government is more than willing to equip them for the task. However, like any military campaign law enforcement additionally require intelligence on the enemy.

The Department of Homeland Security and Intelligence Fusion Centres

Intelligence is a vital asset to any war effort, a notion well-understood by surveillance agencies within the U.S. Infamous cases such as the FBI's Counter Intelligence Program (COINTELPRO) have shown that the American government holds few reservations about spying on its citizens. Legislation introduced in the aftermath of 9/11 greatly changed the powers and scope of domestic intelligence gathering. The "Patriot Act" expanded the surveillance capabilities of the Department of Justice, justified on the grounds of counter terrorism and national security (Bentley, 2012). The Homeland Security Act formed the DHS in 2002 by combining 22 federal agencies underneath the authority of a new cabinet position. Charged with a mission of national security through the prevention of further terrorist attacks the DHS began an aggressive campaign to bolster the defensive capabilities of civilian agencies. Aid came in the form of the material assets already discussed as well as the development of an extensive intelligence sharing apparatus.

In response to criticisms over the failure of government agencies to correlate data connecting hijackers to the plot prior to the attacks on 9/11, intelligence fusion centres coordinated efforts between state and local public agencies to aggregate regional data. Prior to the systemic reformation of the intelligence community that followed 9/11, only two jurisdictions operated fusion centres (Lahneman, 2012). As of 2010, there were at least 72 state and local sites across the U.S., heavily subsidized through DHS grants (Monahan, 2010–2011, p. 84). These sites collect information from countless sources including all levels of law enforcement, branches of the Department of Defense, private corporations, as well as the Central Intelligence Agency (Monahan, 2010–2011). Operated and developed by regional authorities, fusion centres receive additional support from intelligence analysts supplied by the DHS, FBI, and the private sector. Monahan and Palmer (2009) show that data processed includes suspicious activity reports provided to tip hot lines, personal data generated by cell phone use and the Internet, and information generated by other regional databases. They further elaborate that, for example, suspicious activity that requires reporting by officers in the Los Angles Police Department includes the use of binoculars, taking notes, and the espousing of extremist views (Monahan & Palmer, 2009, p. 629). Much emphasis is placed on the collection of digital personal data; one private sector partner with regional intelligence fusion centres boasts having 12 billion records on approximately 98% of the American population (Monahan, 2010–11, p. 87). Telecommunications companies have been shown by Monahan and Palmer to have illegally given customers' personal information to the National Security Agency, an act that the companies in question received retroactive immunity for from legislative amendments passed in the Foreign Intelligence Surveillance Act of 2008 (2009, p. 618). A report on intelligence fusion centres prepared by the American Civil Liberties Union highlights that such sites actively purchase subscriptions to access private sector databases containing unlisted phone numbers, credit reports, and information collected from social networking websites (German & Stanley, 2007, p. 12). From this data mining, "threat profiles" are generated by analysts looking for suspicious trends in persons' buying habits, political interests, and affiliations.

The threat assessments generated by fusion centres enable extensive political and racial profiling by the security state which is then followed up by on the ground investigations. One such operation in Maryland included the sustained surveillance of peace activists and anti-death penalty advocacy organizations for months followed by a covert investigation and infiltration of these groups by law enforcement; this is despite officers reporting no signs of violent intent or activity throughout the course of the investigation (Monahan, 2010–2011, p. 89).The activists under surveillance were then listed in federal databases under suspicion of antigovernment related terrorist activity. Through the application of the terrorist label the state is able to try and further marginalize subversion by setting the parameters of acceptable political expression. As is evident in the threat assessments generated by fusion centres, acceptable expression increasingly excludes forms of advocacy and criticism of state policy.

Targeting anarchist networks has become increasingly salient to the investigations of the DHS. The Missouri Information Analysis Center (MIAC) produced a strategic report on anarchist movements and their activities made up largely of open source data (see MIAC, 2008). Despite a heading informing readers that the report should not serve as the basis for further investigations, the MIAC document concluded that:

> "The MIAC is aware of a number of anarchist networks within Missouri. With their past clashes with the white supremacist movements in our area, we believed it to be important for all Law Enforcement Officers to be aware of the many ideologies and splinter groups that are present within the anarchist movement. Although they have not all been listed, we believe the groups discussed pose a significant domestic terrorist treat at this time". (MIAC, 2008, p. 5)

Groups detailed in the MIAC report include Cop Watch, a non-interventionist police counter surveillance organization, and Anti-Racist Action, a decentralized anti-fascist and anti-racist activist group. This report shows the links law enforcement make between certain forms of political organizing and terrorist activity. Regardless of whether or not organizations like those listed in the MIAC report do break laws in their activities, to conflate their actions as domestic terrorism is the expression of institutionalized political will designed to marginalize and isolate particular types of political behaviour. The label of "terrorist" designates an enemy for law enforcement to pursue; attacking terrorism provides ample justification for pre-emptive aggression and heavy-handed prosecution. In the age of the War on Terror, to be labelled a terrorist is to become an enemy of the U.S. to be met by all the power that such a state can muster. This power, stemming from an integrated intelligence network and a militarized police apparatus, was used by law enforcement in pursuing the Republican National Convention Welcoming Committee in St. Paul and will undoubtedly be used again in the future.

Proactive Suppression:
The 2008 Republican National Convention

In 2006, delegates selected St. Paul, Minnesota, and the city's Excel Energy Center as the location for the Republican National Convention (RNC). In response to the announcement of the convention, on February 14, 2007, a statement was released by an umbrella organization formed of different activist groups known as the RNC Welcoming Committee (RNC-WC). The RNC-WC and their many allies promised civil disobedience to what they perceived as the imposition of the convention on the city as well as to the systemic political and economic injustices emblematic of the RNC. Quoted almost in its entirety below, the initial call to action made by the RNC-WC provides a glimpse into their motivation and actions.

"RNC Welcoming Committee Call Feb 14, 2007:

"Every four years, in two very lucky cities, big money gets thrown around while look-alikes from opposite ends of a closed circle step up to their podiums and spout nonsense. RNC. DNC. Whatever. The point is that once the conventions are over, once November is come and gone, once the inauguration is only an unpleasant memory, people across this stolen land find themselves in pretty much the same place as before: a bad one.

"And we'd like to offer up a movement—some real, tangible change. Unfortunately, the reality is that we're rundown at best, hopeless at worst, and though we see liberation shining off in the distance, we don't know how to get there.

"But we want justice, and we want freedom, for life everywhere. And we're tired of spinning our wheels in this rut.

"From September 1st through 4th, 2008, the Republican National Convention will be held in St. Paul, MN. You can expect the usual: sign-holding, protest marches, rhythm-less chants, false raid scares at the convergence space.

"But damned if the resistance stops there.

"As residents of the Twin Cities, as anti-authoritarians and anarchists, we, the RNC Welcoming Committee invite folks from all over the country to show up and make something happen. Pull this movement out of its rut, or start something new. Let the up-tops know that we could give a shit about their suits, their speeches, their money. Bring your (A)-game, cause 2008 is ours". (Republican National Convention Welcoming Committee [RNC-WC], 2007)

Nearly a year later statements made on the RNC-WC's website by an affiliate, Unconventional Action, openly called for civil disobedience and direct actions against transportation routes into the St. Paul. This new call came in the wake of national consultation organized by the RNC-WC to discuss strategies and actions leading up to the convention. A consensus had formed around blocking transportation routes into the city of St. Paul as well as forming blockades on roads leading to the Excel Energy Center to prevent delegates from reaching the convention hall (RNC-WC, 2008). All of these statements were issued publicly on the now defunct website nornc.org in an effort to mobilize as many people as possible to come to St. Paul and take part in demonstrations against a convention that symbolized the authority and actions of both the Republican Party and the U.S. government.

The RNC-WC, being an open group organizing a highly publicized protest, was well known to law enforcement agencies and the domestic intelligence apparatus before the protests were to occur. In the lead up to the Republican National Convention numerous agencies coordinated an extensive surveillance campaign to identify supposed threats and create a security plan. Highway Watch, a private-public intelligence fusion centre that worked in conjunction with the Department of Homeland Security and the Transportation Security Agency wrote a report entitled "Plans to Target Transportation Infrastructure Surrounding Republican National Convention" published a little over a year after the RNC-WC's initial call out in February. The report detailed information largely available to the public: the RNC-WC had already published on their website maps of St. Paul and Unconventional Action's statement of intent to disrupt transportation routes during the convention (Highway Watch, 2008). The report also featured commentary on the RNC-WC's tongue-in-cheek press release of their intent to purchase hundreds of tasers for their members, financed by raiding weapons manufacturers. This mirrored official statements made by St. Paul's police of the department's purchase of over one hundred tasers that would arrive just in time for the RNC: a fact which the police claimed was simple coincidence and in no way in response to the upcoming protests, asserting that the tasers were simply for the protection of their officers. Despite acknowledging the lack of any evidence showing that the RNC-WC's had the material means to purchase such weapons, as well as a failure to understand the sarcastic criticism of the police's action levied in the press release, Highway Watch cautioned law enforcement to take notice of the announcement.

The report by Highway Watch (2008) provides insight into the mentality of law enforcement and their partner agencies: one of heightened paranoia over the perceived threat that anarchists posed to the Republican National Convention. Highway Watch detailed a crude social network analysis based on digital links between the websites used by activist groups to share information and organize. Groups with high amounts of "between-ness," determined by the number of informal links between groups, were seen as central hubs of anarchist organizing. The RNC-WC ranked in the report as the most centralized node of the various groups participating in protests against the national political convention, followed by the Democratic Party convention counterpart DNC Disruption 08 and by Unconventional Action, a group that would be present at both convention protests. The Highway Watch report illustrates the comprehension intelligence agencies have of decentralized organizational strategies' efficacy in opposition to surveillance and state repression, as well as their views of such tactics:

> "Consequently, these networks are more difficult to disrupt due to their loose connections and easy ability to replace damaged or compromised nodes. As such, the national convention anarchists are following the pattern of most terror networks in this aspect". (Highway Watch, 2008)

By equating the structure of the RNC-WC to that of a terrorist cell, Highway Watch and the Department of Homeland Security explicitly link the politics of anarchism with those of terrorism. In doing so, they prey upon some of the deepest fears that intelligence and law enforcement communities possess; those of more terrorist attacks on American soil. This decontextualizes the reasons behind the RNC-WC's desire to protest the political convention and then provides justification for the further criminalization of dissent; the anarchists organize just like terrorists and terrorists are the enemy in the current war.

Two days before the start of the convention police conducted a pre-emptive raid on a convergence centre used by the RNC-WC. In an affidavit filed by investigators police alleged that the RNC-WC was an organized, criminal conspiracy intent on using violent, destructive acts to disrupt the convention. The affidavit cited official investigations that were heavily reliant on the testimony of undercover police infiltration and paid criminal informants who detailed alleged criminal plots including blockading techniques with lock boxes, using slingshots and throwing rocks to target police, and tactics to free arrested colleagues (Samec, Sommerhause & Clark, 2008). Informants were able to gain access to the RNC-WC's email list-serv and attended pre-RNC civil disobedience training events organized by groups affiliated to, but separate from, the RNC-WC. At these training events it was alleged that activists practised guerrilla warfare tactics such as building and using Molotov cocktails and overturning cars to form barricades. Informants cited in the affidavit further alleged that persons listed on the warrant request had expressed interest in purchasing firearms and that there were guns in the space (Samec, Sommerhause, & Clark, 2008). Heavily armed police raided the convergence centre and detained dozens of activists while other officers executed search warrants for everything from bomb making materials to collected urine and feces supposedly to be used in attacking police.

The receipt for the raid listed no improvised explosive devices, no weapons, nor buckets of urine. What police listed as confiscated were thousands of fliers, sign-making supplies such as paint, numerous boxes labelled on the receipt as "anarchist political literature," as well personal electronics including cell phones, cameras, and laptops (Samec, Sommerhause, & Clark, 2008). Police then interrogated and photographed activists staying in the centre. Preemptive raids continued throughout St. Paul and the surrounding area targeting homes used by the RNC-WC as well as allied groups including the Food Not Bombs and I-Witness Video, resulting in mass detentions but few actual arrests (Fisher, 2010). In all cases police seized electronic equipment and political literature.

In total eight organizers of the RNC-WC were arrested during other pre-emptive raids before the Republican National Convention. Known collectively as the RNC-8, the activists were first charged under the *Minnesota Patriot Act of 2002* with allegations of Conspiracy to Commit Riot in the Second Degree in the Furtherance of Terrorism (State of Minnesota, County of Ramsey, 2008). The charges of Conspiracy to Commit Criminal Damage to Property in the First Degree in Furtherance of Terrorism was added later that year in addition to the criminal complaint made by prosecutors; months after the convention had finished (State of Minnesota, County of Ramsey, 2009). The same charges had also been applied to each of the accused without the terrorism designation, effectively charging each defendant for the same alleged offence twice, for a total of four charges per arrestee. Conviction under anti-terrorist legislation would have carried additional sentencing extensions, however the charges filed under the *Minnesota Patriot Act of 2002* were dismissed in 2009 by the state because, "under the circumstances, the terrorism charge just complicates the case" (Office of the Ramsey County Attorney, 2009). By 2010, the trials against the RNC-8 had been resolved: three of the defendants had their charges dropped while the five other accused made plea deals with prosecutors resulting in sentences of probation, community service, and for a single member of the accused 91 days in a county workhouse.

Conclusion

The Republican National Conventions illustrates the criminalization of dissent and the militarization of law enforcement. Through fusions of federal, state, and local police with private enterprises, the state's security apparatus attempted to pre-emptively identify, infiltrate, and disrupt the activities of not only anarchists, but of all associated organizations that joined the convergence in St. Paul in protest of the RNC. The application of the *Minnesota Patriot Act* in the charges filed against the RNC-8 exposes how the U.S. government has utilized legislation created to fight terrorism to try to isolate and alienate political dissidents. By utilizing a discourse of terrorism the government warrants a heavily militarized and pre-emptive response to harass and disrupt popular campaigns for civil disobedience. Brutality and excessive force are in turn justified by the requirements of a War on Terror. Had the Ramsey County courts secured convictions under the banner of terrorism legislature the state would then have had further legal support for their invasive campaigns countering political dissent.

Through criminalizing the RNC-8 and anarchism as a political philosophy the government explicitly places limits on what beliefs are acceptable for public expression. This reality is not limited solely to major events such as political conventions. Increasingly, any challengers to the status quo would bear the brunt of a police force trained and equipped for a high-intensity conflict, bulwarked by a legal system tailor crafted to isolate dissidence, and reinforced by an extensive network of surveillance and infiltration that categorizes beliefs and behaviour into neat, essentialized, mythical threats.

References

Bentley, E. (2012). Homeland Security Law and Policy. In K. G. Logan & J. D. Ramsay (Eds.), *Introduction to Homeland Security* (pp. 19–46). Boulder, CO: Westview Press.

Brown, C. A. (2011). Divided Loyalties: Ethical Challenges for America's Law Enforcement in Post 9/11 America. *Case Western Reserve Journal of International Law*, 43(3), 651–675.

Coburn, T. (2012). *Safety at Any Price: Assessing the Impact of Homeland Security Spending in U.S. Cities*. Washington, DC: Office of Senator Tom Coburn, Member, Homeland Security and Governmental Affairs Committee. December.
http://www.coburn.senate.gov/public//index.cfm?a=Files.Serve&File_i d=b86fdaeb-86ff-4d19-a112-415ec85aa9b6

Fisher, J. (2010). *SWAT Madness and the Militarization of the American Police: A National Dilemma*. Santa Barbra, CA: ABC-CLIO.

German, M., & Stanley, J. (2007). *What's Wrong with Fusion Centres?* New York, NY: American Civil Liberties Union.
https://www.aclu.org/sites/default/files/pdfs/privacy/fusioncenter_200 71212.pdf

Graeber, D. (2013). *The Democracy Project: A History, a Crisis, a Movement*. New York, NY: Penguin Books.

Hill, S., & Berger, R. (2009). A Paramilitary Policing Juggernaut. *Social Justice*, 36(1), 25–40.

Highway Watch. (2008). Plans to Target Transportation Infrastructure Surrounding Republican National Convention. Department of Homeland Security: Transportation Security Operations Center (TSOC).
http://wlstorage.net/file/dhs-rnc-transport-infra-2008.pdf

Kraska, P. B. (2007). Militarization and Policing: Its Relevance to 21st Century Police. *Policing*,1(4), 501–512.
http://cjmasters.eku.edu/sites/cjmasters.eku.edu/files/21stmilitarizati on.pdf

Kraska, P. B., & Kappeler, V. E. (1997). Militarizing American Police: The Rise and Normalization of Paramilitary Units. *Social Problems*, 44(1), 1–18.

Lahneman, W. J. (2012). Homeland Security Intelligence. In K. G. Logan & J. D. Ramsay (Eds.), *Introduction to Homeland Security* (pp. 97–124). Boulder, CO: Westview Press.

Missouri Intelligence Analysis Center (MIAC). (2008). MIAC Strategic Report: Anarchist Movement. Jefferson City, MO: Division of Drug & Crime Control.

http://info.publicintelligence.net/MIAC-Anarchists.pdf

Monahan, T. (2010–2011). The Future of Security? Operations at Homeland Security Fusion Centres. *Social Justice*, 37(2/3), 84–98.

Monahan, T., & Palmer, N. A. (2009). The Emerging Politics of DHS Fusion Centers. *Security Dialogue*, 40(6), 617–636.

Office of the Ramsey County Attorney. (2009). "Terrorism" Counts against 8 RNC Defendants to Be Dismissed; Other Conspiracy Charges Remain [Press release].
http://minnesota.publicradio.org/features/2009/04/09_newscut_rncrele ase/8_RNC_Defendants.pdf

Republican National Convention Welcoming Committee (RNC-WC). (2007). Welcoming Committee Statement.
http://web.archive.org/web/20080906105257/http://www.nornc.org/167 /

———— . (2008). Crash the Convention: Call to Action.
http://web.archive.org/web/20080907081250/http://www.nornc.org

Samec, T.; Sommerhause, D.; & Clark, R. (2008). RNC-WC Convergence Center Warrant.

State of Minnesota and County of Ramsey. (2008). State of Minnesota vs Eryn Trimmer and co defendants. Count Attorney Complaint No: 2073788-1.
http://www.minnpost.com/sites/default/files/asset/d/d2b624/d2b624.pd f

State of Minnesota and County of Ramsey. (2009). State of Minnesota vs Luce Guillen-Givins and co defendants. Count Attorney Complaint No:2073787-3.
http://stmedia.startribune.com/documents/GuillenGivinsLuce.pdf

CHAPTER FIVE

Echoes of Eisenhower:
The U.S. and the War for Profit

Julian Stasky

In 1961 Former President Dwight D. Eisenhower gave a moving speech highlighting the immense dangers of the military-industrial complex. Citing its insidious nature, Eisenhower warned the American population of the deleterious effects of the marriage of military industry and government. Fast forward 50 years, and Eisenhower takes on the stature of a Nostradamus. His prescient concerns have never been more relevant than they are today. The intention of this chapter is to explore the current military-industry complex and its place within the United States of America. I will first explore the war wage, a WWII creation, and its role in building the military-industrial complex (MIC). Then I will demonstrate the immense hold that the MIC has on the U.S. government and economy with its astronomical defense spending which is exponentially outpacing the rest of the world. I will investigate Halliburton's privileged place amongst contractors, and highlight the characteristics that make it the epitome of a corporation deeply entwined in the MIC. The effects that current global political economy will likely have on the U.S.' hegemonic tendencies are also addressed here. Finally, I will briefly explore the future of the American government and economy in light of the stranglehold that defense spending has on its health.

The War Wage and the Military-Industrial Complex

Shrouded by its very nature, the MIC's origin cannot be traced to a specific point in time. In its most basic form, it has existed since modern industrialization took hold. Once mass production was possible, it was only logical that it would be used to produce weapons of war as well as implements of peace. The initial thrust of the complex into the public consciousness came from the oration of Dwight Eisenhower, warning of the dangers inherent in the entanglement of war industry and government.

The development of the "war wage" involved a WWII campaign by industry and the government to "fully integrate workers' and civilians' lives into the war effort" (Vitale, 2011). This war wage focused on tenets not dissimilar from those used in armed forces recruiting: "a sense of contribution, national belonging, and sacrifice". The war wage allowed government and industry, with the support of the people, to transform the economy and devote significantly more resources to the production of war materials. This represented a significant victory for both military industry and the government, as it co-opted the average American into the fight, galvanizing the public against a common enemy and ensuring that United States would never be short of necessary accoutrements of war.

The U.S.: An Economy Built on Defense

Though the marriage of the Department of Defense with private industry dates back at least half a century, the prevalence of the MIC within all aspects of life and government in the U.S. is a relatively recent phenomenon. The nation was built on a foundation of war; in the last 200 years, instances of the use of U.S. armed forces abroad numbers in the hundreds, with semantic issues and secret missions making a definitive count impossible (Grimmett, 2004). Seizing on the national ethos of "America, f--- yeah", the defense industry has sown its roots deep into the fabric of American life. After a decade of decreasing defense spending, the base defense budget has nearly doubled since 2001, rising from $287 billion to a staggering $530 billion in 2012; more than the spending of the next 13 nations *combined*. Additionally, this number does not include any of the primary costs attributed to the wars in Iraq and Afghanistan, which would skyrocket this figure from enormous to incomprehensible. Defense accounts for approximately 20% of the

United States' total spending and a whopping 58% of its discretionary spending (Plumer, 2013; Ananda, 2013).

As the U.S. continues to struggle in the wake of the "Great Recession" and a sluggish, supposed recovery, defense industry proponents are once again on the defensive. Balancing the national budget, a herculean task to be sure, naturally requires compromises across the board. Defense contractors are hoping they can sit this one out. In an attempt to preserve valuable tax dollars for their clients, the rhetoric from lobbyists and politicians alike is shifting. Where national security was once the end for the means of prolific defense spending, the conversation has now turned to economics, and more specifically, jobs. In a 2011 press conference, then Defense Secretary Leon Panetta and Joint Chiefs of Staff Chairman Mike Mullen emphasized "that soldiers and civilians who work in and around the defense community are employees who rely on a paycheck just like the rest of Americans" (Rasor, 2011). While this statement is not without merit, the actual jobs numbers are a subject of considerable debate. Todd Harrison of the Center for Strategic and Budgetary Assessments contends that the U.S Department of Defense is the largest single employer in the country, putting more Americans to work than Wal-Mart and the Postal Service combined. CNN reports that the defense budget pays for "3.1 million employees, both military and civilian" and that "another 3 million people are employed by the defense industry" directly or indirectly (Rizzo, 2011). In contrast, a report compiled by the auditing and financial consulting firm Deloitte states that in 2010 the Department of Defense directly employed about one million people, with another 2.5 million being employed indirectly (Pianin, 2012). With figures as disparate as 6.1 million and 3.5 million, it is no wonder that Pentagon spending watchdog Winslow Wheeler is skeptical about official government numbers:

> "You have multiplier effects for the Burger King down by the manufacturing plant and the dry cleaner that is being supported by the revenue flowing into the community....If you use the secondary and tertiary jobs from transportation and education spending you can run up the numbers, too, but if you talk about direct labor jobs that the money creates, that is quite different". (Rizzo, 2011)

Furthermore, a recent study done at the University of Massachusetts at Amherst concluded that "$1 billion spent on clean energy, health care or education would do far more for job creation than $1 billion spent by the Pentagon" (Pollin & Garrett-Peltier,

2011, p. 1), further undermining the argument for maintaining current levels of defense spending. While a single study does not a new policy make, it is clear that there is significant disagreement concerning the economic impact of the Department of Defense.

Halliburton: A Case Study

If one was ever looking for a company which epitomizes corporate greed and the MIC, Halliburton is it. Founded in 1919 by Erle P. Halliburton, it started as a business cementing oil wells. Today Halliburton operates in 80 countries, employing 72,000 people, and in 2012 had a net income of $2.6 billion dollars (Halliburton, 2012, 2013). Due to its heavy involvement in the Iraq War, both in support for U.S. forces and reconstruction, Halliburton provides us with an excellent case study to examine the inner workings of the military-industrial complex.

In 2003, spurred by erroneous reports of weapons of mass destruction, the U.S. violated the sovereignty of Iraq and invaded, ostensibly to depose embattled dictator Saddam Hussein. Government officials, all the way up to President George W. Bush, valiantly tried to convince the American public that this was a war to remove a brutal dictator, one who had used chemical weapons in the past (true), currently had some of said chemical weapons in his arsenal (false), and was a significant threat to the national security of the U.S. (egregiously false). Without support from Congress, the American people, or the global community, the U.S. barreled into what would turn out to be one of the most unmitigated disasters in the history of U.S. foreign interventions.

In order to wage a war on the scale that the Iraq conflict required, the U.S. needed more bodies; they simply did not have enough soldiers to maintain an adequately sized fighting force alongside support operations. Thus, Iraq became the war of contractors. In the last decade, the U.S. has handed out $138 billion taxpayer dollars to a wide variety of military contractors. The top ten companies combined received 52% of the funds, with $39.5 billion (28.6% of total funds) going to one company: Kellogg, Brown, and Root (KBR). KBR was a subsidiary of Halliburton until it was sold in 2007. These moneys were awarded via the Logistics Civil Augmentation Program (LOGCAP). The LOGCAP is responsible for running forward operating bases, and dispenses services ranging from the dining facilities, to laundry, to the gym (Haynes, 2011).

In 2009, the Office of the Special Inspector for Iraq Reconstruction prepared a report detailing the history of LOGCAP contracts. According to the report, LOGCAP grew from a down-sizing of the military post-Vietnam. Following what was becoming a global trend, the U.S. Army began outsourcing an array of responsibilities in the war effort. The sheer size of the contractor force in Iraq is remarkable: by comparison the report notes that, "in World War II, one contractor was deployed for every seven soldiers. During the 2003 invasion, that number had increased to one for every 2.4. By 2006, contractors outnumbered soldiers in Iraq" (Holan, 2010).

Unfortunately for the taxpayer, in taking on a conflict of such complexity, the U.S. failed to ensure proper oversight for the awarding and execution of contracts in the Middle East. In fact, KBR has been implicated in overcharging and defrauding the U.S. government to the tune of hundreds of millions of dollars. While many of the claims are for relatively small sums (millions rather than billions), the nature of the deception is alarming. In 2008, KBR was awarded a contract worth $5 million a year to repair all manner of tactical vehicles at Joint Base Balad north of Baghdad. A Pentagon report reveals that 144 civilian mechanics were hired by KBR and each subsequently worked an infinitesimal 43 minutes a month. KBR was paid in full regardless of the fact that they completed less than 7% of their expected work (Weinstein, 2010). In another case, the Department of Justice is suing KBR for improperly billing the "Army more than $48.7 million for a subcontractor's inflated and unauthorized costs while providing housing trailers for troops in Iraq" (Tomasko, 2012). Most disturbing of all is KBR's implication in human trafficking. According to one report, "about 1,000 Asian men who were hired by a Kuwaiti subcontractor to the U.S. military have been confined for as long as three months in windowless warehouses near the Baghdad airport without money or a place to work" (Ashton, 2008). The laborers each paid $2,000 to middle men and were promised jobs in Iraq that would pay $600 to $800 a month. That work still has not come.

These are but a few examples of the corruption that war-profiteering engenders. Corporations such as Halliburton take advantage of the chaos of war to fleece the American government of millions of dollars. Dan Goure, vice-president of the Lexington Institute, has stated that the "the US had created a fifth branch of the military....It's called the private sector" (Fifield, 2013). According to a 2011 report from the commission on Wartime Contracting in Iraq and Afghanistan, approximately $60 billion has been lost to waste or fraud since 2001, a staggering $12 million *per day*. Furthermore, as combat troops withdrew from Iraq, contractors stayed behind. The State Department has estimated that it will pay $3 billion over the next five years solely on private security contracts meant to protect the indefensibly large embassy in Baghdad.

Hegemony in Trouble

The U.S., in the quest to retain global supremacy, must radically alter the strategy of "might makes right". With the availability of information exploding at an exponential rate, countries can no longer illegitimately hide behind a guise of humanitarian intervention to invade those it does not agree with, as we can see with the significant public resistance to continuing the wars in the Middle East or getting involved in new conflicts. As the U.S. tightens its fiscal belt, they must make hard choices about the future of their foreign policy. Currently, the U.S. maintains over 1,000 military installations around the globe, in addition to 4,000 more at home (Turse, 2011). They use this vast array of resources to maintain their influence in every corner of the globe. However, the retention of all of these bases in light of what will likely be a reduction in finances seems impossible. Bases will close, personnel will be called back from deployment, and the presence of the most powerful nation this planet has ever seen will begin to fade. Obviously, this will not entail a monumental reduction in foreign presence, but it will no doubt be significant. The question then becomes, can the U.S. continue to maintain its current status quo, from foreign policy to decisions on discretionary spending, in this ever-evolving political, social, and economic climate? I would argue that although they may attempt to hold on to their hegemonic aspirations for as long as possible, the sooner they rid themselves of what is clearly an impossible dream, the easier the transition will be to their role as a post-imperialist superpower.

Reflections

It is readily apparent that the U.S. has finagled itself into an untenable situation. Running concurrent to the increased xenophobic tensions around the world is a global recession, adversely affecting even the most powerful of nations. The U.S., in a nod to its historically hegemonic nature, is vainly attempting to maintain its status on the global stage. To compensate for waning democratic influence, the U.S. has continued to build its military might, hoping to intimidate rather than negotiate. Much to its dismay, this behavior appears unsustainable. With national debt at record highs and dismal job numbers that are unlikely to significantly improve anytime soon, the citizenry is clamoring for change. Though the Department of Defense employs a significant number of Americans, they have demonstrated time and time again that they are inefficient at best. The two wars of the past decade have caused untold damage to the national fabric of the U.S. Not only have they contributed to spiraling debt, they have cost thousands of lives. It is this last point that I believe is so often overlooked. When war becomes a business, and calculations are done in dollars rather than lives, the very soul of a nation degrades. When the concern is not for lives put in danger or loved ones lost but for an unquenchable thirst for higher profits, society can only suffer.

References

Ananda, R. (2013). More than 50% of US Government Spending Goes to the Military. *GlobalResearch.ca*, March 27.
http://www.globalresearch.ca/more-than-50-of-us-government-spending-goes-to-the-military/18852

Ashton, A. (2008). Military Contractor in Iraq Holds Foreign Workers in Warehouses. *McClatchy Newspapers*, December 2.
http://www.mcclatchydc.com/2008/12/02/56910/military-contractor-in-iraq-holds.html

Fifield, A. (2013). Contractors Reap $138 billion from Iraq War, Cheney's Halliburton #1 with $39.5 Billion. *Financial Times*, March 18.
http://www.ft.com/intl/cms/s/0/7f435f04-8c05-11e2-b001-00144feabdc0.html#axzz2Pvr16ZB8

Grimmett, R. F. (2004)."Instances of Use of United States Armed Forces Abroad, 1798–2004. *CRS Report RL30172*.
http://www.au.af.mil/au/awc/awcgate/crs/rl30172.htm

Haynes, M. G. (2011). LOGCAP Demystified: A Primer on LOGCAP Services. *Army Sustainment*, 43(6), 44–47.

Halliburton. (2012). Annual Report 2012.
http://ir.halliburton.com/phoenix.zhtml?c=67605&p=irol-irhome

Halliburton. (2013). History of Halliburton.
http://www.halliburton.com/aboutus/default.aspx?navid=970&pageid=2312

Holan, A. D. (2010). Halliburton, KBR, and Iraq War contracting: A History So Far. *Tampa Bay Times/Politifact*, June 6.

http://www.politifact.com/truth-o-
meter/statements/2010/jun/09/arianna-huffington/halliburton-kbr-
and-iraq-war-contracting-history-s/

Pianin, E. (2012). The Pentagon Mantra: Cut Defense, Slaughter Jobs. *The Fiscal Times*, July 24.

http://www.thefiscaltimes.com/Articles/2012/07/24/The-Pentagon-
Mantra-Cut-Defense-Slaughter-Jobs.aspx#chtL3DS3BpT4ivtL.99

Plumer, B. (2013). America's Staggering Defense Budget, in Charts. *The Washington Post*, January 7.

http://www.washingtonpost.com/blogs/wonkblog/wp/2013/01/07/everyt
hing-chuck-hagel-needs-to-know-about-the-defense-budget-in-charts/

Pollin, R., & Garrett-Peltier, H. (2011). *The U.S. Employment Effects of Military and Domestic Spending Priorities: 2011 Update*. Amherst, MA: Department of Economics and Political Economy Research Institute (PERI),University of Massachusetts-Amherst.

http://www.peri.umass.edu/fileadmin/pdf/published_study/PERI_milit
ary_spending_2011.pdf

Rasor, D. (2011). Defense Spending: The Worst Way to Make Jobs. *Truthout*, September 7.

http://www.truth-out.org/opinion/item/3166:defense-spending-the-
worst-way-to-make-jobs

Rizzo, J. (2011). Defense Cuts: The Jobs Numbers Game. *CNN: Security Clearance*, September 22.

http://security.blogs.cnn.com/2011/09/22/defense-cuts-the-jobs-
numbers-game/

Tomasko, C. (2012). KBR Committed $48.7 Million Fraud on Iraq Housing Job, U.S. Says. *Thomson Reuters*, December 10.

http://blog.thomsonreuters.com/index.php/kbr-committed-48-7-
million-fraud-on-iraq-housing-job-u-s-says/

Turse, N. (2011). Tomgram: Nick Turse, the Pentagon's Planet of Bases. *TomDispatch*, January 9.

http://www.tomdispatch.com/blog/175338/

Vitale, P. (2011). Wages of War: Manufacturing nationalism during World War II. *Antipode*, 43(3), 783-819.

Weinstein, A. (2010). KBR Bills $5 Million for Mechanics Who Work 43 Minutes a Month. *Mother Jones*, March 25.

http://www.motherjones.com/politics/2010/03/kbr-idle-hands-iraq-
balad-contract-waste-pentagon-report-hearing

CHAPTER SIX

Spectacular War: Media, Militainment, and the New Imperialism

Philip Capozzi

ollowing the events of 9/11, the U.S. media went through a transformation, bringing together war, media, and entertainment closer than they ever had been before. The media have the power to set the agenda in terms of the information that we are to see, hear, and read on a daily basis. What gets broadcast on television and in movies, published in newsprint, and heard on the radio can affects audiences in many (different) ways. As a result there is much research done in the field of media studies, sociology, and communication studies in order to understand the effects that media has on its audiences. However, this transformation of U.S. media brought many other interesting concepts to the foreground that merits just as much analysis and study. Throughout this paper how media affects populations will not be the main focus, as this field is very broad and much evidence is inconclusive. Rather, this amalgamation of war, media, and entertainment and how American imperialist efforts forced this process is of central focus.

When discussing imperialism some may be tempted think only of fifteenth- and sixteenth-century Europe, when powerful European countries, such as Great Britain and Spain, expanded around the world setting up trade routes and creating colonies to extract raw materials. As time passed and colonies started fighting for their independence, many questioned if imperialism still existed. According to David Harvey (2003), we have entered the age of new imperialism, which consists of the U.S.' battle for the control of world economy through the way West knows best: the military. Some American efforts that have come to define this new imperialism are the U.S.' fight for the control of oil, which has a direct link to the control of world economy, and its intervention in many Middle Eastern countries, including outright occupation, under the guise of bringing democracy.

In 2003, U.S. media broadcasted on live television the bombing of Baghdad, part of the "shock and awe" strategy, which was full of bright flashes and sounds of explosions, described by many reporters as an "incredible light show" reminiscent of a movie trailer or a fireworks show (Stahl, 2007). It was not just a military strike but also a televised event that was filmed with cameras that had been set up in advance. These new imperialist efforts in part gave rise to the coming together of war, media and entertainment, or, more succinctly referred to by Roger Stahl as *militainment*. As an extension of older phenomena, such as psychological operations (PSYOP), propaganda, and "public relations", militainment is defined as "war packaged for pleasurable consumption" (Stahl, 2007) as well as the "cooperation between the military and the media and culture industry on an everyday basis that goes beyond war and crisis" (Thomas, 2009, p. 106). It is the acceptance of war images as a source of entertainment either through movies, television programming, video games, or news. Many news reporters are embedded with the soldiers, meaning they wear soldiers' uniforms and follow the army on their missions, in order to report their stories. Through this process of "embedding", however, the Pentagon is able to push its agenda in order for the reporters to gain access to the ranks of the military, which ends up producing a sanitized, not to mention authorized, image of war (Ignatius, 2010; Wells, 2003, Hewitt, n.d.). Furthermore, many major news networks are owned by military contractors, such as NBC which was owned by General Electric until it was acquired by Comcast in 2011. These recent "shock and awe" spectacles coupled with war movies and television shows help blur the lines between "real" war images and war images that are digitally enhanced. America's new imperialist efforts have created a shift toward militainment in order to gain support for its military campaigns through recruitment, perform counterinsurgency measures, and by normalizing American military action as a legitimate and just way of solving "world problems".

Effects of Imperialism on Media at Home

The military, media, and entertainment have formed a close relationship in recent years, which can be seen in the amount of war-related images being broadcast. War, occupation, and any other imperialist activity give rise to violence, civilian death, civilian displacement, and many other social and physical atrocities, all of which the American government, especially the Pentagon, wishes to downplay. The media disseminates a message of a "clean" war, which makes light of the violence by showing a "faceless" enemy with no real images of death (Stahl, 2007). Furthermore, these images are tailored to reinforce a positive message about the military in an effort to gain support and recruitment. In order to understand the effects imperialism has on the media, it is important to consider how the Pentagon is able to control the content of movies and television shows, and how imperialist efforts dictate the media content abroad.

The Pentagon is extremely demanding when it comes to portraying the American military in the media. Only images of valiant soldiers saving the day, soldiers liberating oppressed people, and messages of freedom are some of the few allowed forms of representation. The Pentagon has gone to great lengths in order to ensure a neatly packaged depiction of the average American soldier in movies, television shows, and even the news. How is the Pentagon able to achieve this? Doesn't the Second Amendment to the American Constitution protect the freedom of speech allowing any American to represent the military in any way they want?

Anytime a filmmaker or producer wants to make a movie involving anything to do with army equipment, such as planes, helicopters, guns, tank, etc, they can either rent or create the equipment themselves, which is very costly and time consuming, or they can ask the Pentagon to borrow army supplies, which is much cheaper. However, the latter option comes with an underlying clause. Accepting equipment and funding from the Pentagon means that Phil Strub[1], the head of the Pentagon's film liaison office at the Department of Defense in Washington D.C., has full power and authority to change any part of the script or screenplay. This process has become streamlined to the effect of turning movies into virtual infomercials and recruitment posters for the military. Even Strub has said,

> "there's no question that we do things to influence public opinion and to help recruiting and retention. There are no statistics to show a causal relationship, but there are tons of anecdotal evidence. I think there is a consensus of opinion that it does work". (Quoted in Robb, 2004, p. 178)

Any and all negative representations Strub comes across are immediately removed and replaced with more positive representations. This involves anything from changing the dialogue of the characters, to changing entire scenes, and sometimes even changing history. For example, the movie *Windtalkers* starring Nicholas Cage, playing the bodyguard of a code talker, is about the second world war Navaho code talkers that aided in passing coded messages, which the Japanese were never able to break, that allowed the Americans to take Iwo Jima and secure victory. In this movie many scenes and dialogues were changed in favor of a positive military image. One scene in particular that caused an uproar when the Pentagon attempted to change it was the scene involving Cage's character getting a direct order to kill his code talker in the event of imminent capture. Although this scene was based on historical facts, backed up by many veteran Navaho code talkers, Strub and the Pentagon had their own version of history (Robb, 2004, p. 63). In the end the Pentagon got its way and the scene was changes so that Cage's character no longer received direct orders to kill his code talker, it was only subtly implied. Changes such as these, however, have led to some, such as screenwriter Darryl Ponicsan, calling this process "clearly a form of censorship" (Robb, 2004, p. 47).

The events of certain episodes of the television show *The West Wing* are used as a case study by Davidson (2006) to show how the soft power (the ability to persuade) of Hollywood creates a suspicious and militarized cultural consciousness about "Muslim" societies during the events of the "War on Terror" and how it affected U.S.-Turkish relationships. Davidson rejects all notions that the soft power of Hollywood is separate from the hard power (military and financial) of the state using militainment as an example. The episode's events entailed a suicide bombing that took place in an Antalya, Turkey movie theatre that killed Americans, Italians, and Turks. Antalya is not seen as a city of many inhabitants existing through many forms of social experience in *The West Wing*. It is only viewed as a site where Americans were killed and as a result gave them cause to invade the Middle East. The only concerns highlighted in the show are those of Americans. By using images of war, the Pentagon, and real news broadcast footage, such as CNN, in *The West Wing,* militainment gains the power to blend hard (Pentagon), medium (CNN), and soft (*The West Wing*) powers together and broadcasts it all at prime time. This example given by Davidson further shows how the Pentagon is able to control the media in order to create a positive representation in their favor while gaining support for their imperialist efforts.

Imperialism and U.S. Media Abroad

If the Pentagon is able to change the images in the local media in order to create a positive and reinforcing representation of the military, what techniques are employed in order to gain favor and maintain control abroad? Through greater economic power, the U.S., like other rich countries, is able to create its own media content without relying on other countries for filming equipment or information, unlike Third World countries that often import U.S. media equipment and information. This gives U.S. media a greater ability to control foreign broadcasters by controlling the information they receive, which is characteristic of media imperialism. Omoera and Ibagere define media imperialism as the control and/or influence over all things concerning media (ownership, distribution, etc.) in one country by another (2010, p. 2). Furthermore, there are also U.S. government owned and operated media outlets that are aimed at foreign audiences such as Voice of America news, which is one of the subsidiaries of the U.S. international broadcasters' agency the Broadcasting Board of Governors (BBG).

Also there have been a number of cases of CIA and State Department projects of ghostwriting and planting stories in foreign countries, such as the case of Laurie Adler in Iraq. Laurie Adler, according to her LinkedIn profile[2], was the Strategic Communications Advisor, Human Terrain System at US Department of Army from 2007–2008. Working with the Lincoln Group, Adler, who handled public relations, was responsible for using Pentagon funds in order to plant articles written by U.S. military operatives in Iraqi newspapers (Forte, 2008).

The Spectacle of War and "Blurring the Lines"

The consequences of the creative control the Pentagon has on the production of Hollywood movies and television shows, are greater than simply a misrepresentation of the American military. Other than creating support and aiding recruitment for the military, the over abundance of the portrayal of war in film and video games and the effects of ensuring "clean" war images in order to gain compliance has turned war into a spectacle—an event to be watched, enjoyed, and consumed. Through the Pentagon's efforts of turning war into a spectacle creates a binary of humanizing and dehumanizing effects, where Americans are over humanized to engage the viewer in their struggles and triumphs and the enemies are dehumanized, faceless props. War images on television, either real or fictional, are no longer distinguishable: they have become one and the same. Through this spectacularization of war, the Pentagon has been able to, in effect, blur the lines between real war and digitally enhanced war, and between citizen and soldier. This method of blurring the lines reinforces measures of psychological counterinsurgency, increases recruitment, and further normalizes military intervention as the just and only way of solving problems. It makes "let's fight" a normalized mode of conflict resolution and "such representation serves a normative function, producing and disseminating new criteria of citizenship and training individuals to embrace their roles as servants of government, rather than participants in it" (Takacs, 2012, p. 105).

Following the televised event of the Gulf War and by using the film *Apocalypse Now* as an example, Solomon (2007) investigates the way in which the U.S. army wants to depict war as a spectacle—machines battling hard targets—instead of one of human violence. By turning war into a spectacle, it gains a positive spin by removing humanizing aspects distracting Americans from the many soldiers killing and dying overseas, while gaining support for the war all at the same time. The spectacle produces a blurring effect that makes the difference between soldier and civilian, passive observer and active participant, indistinguishable. By reinforcing a tacit consent of imperialism and war, the lines between the images of war shown in the cinema, real or enhanced with special effects, and the actual events on the battlefield become one and the same. Even seemingly anti-war movies, such as *Apocalypse Now*, potentially reinforce our support for imperialism as a result of accepting images of war as a form of entertainment.

Video games also play a big part in turning war into a spectacle, which, in turn, takes the indistinguishability between citizen and soldier, real war images and digitally enhanced, to a next level. Now people are no longer just watching the war, they can actively participate in it from the comfort of their own homes, "providing exposure along the way to the technological marvels of the U.S. military" (Power, 2009, p. 199). Furthermore, "digital war games present a clean, sanitized and enjoyable version of war for popular consumptions, obscuring realities, contexts, and consequences of war. Additionally, digital games provide players with coping strategies in a world full of geopolitical anxiety and uncertainty" (Power, 2009, p. 200).

Roger Stahl (2006) examines war-based video games arguing that they "represent a nexus for the militarization of cultural space," which produces an identity that he calls "virtual citizen-soldier" (p. 113). Stahl argues how the televised views of spectacles such as "Operation Desert Storm" and "shock and awe" led to greater militarization of civilian life, which then translated into other forms of media, such as video games. Expensive vehicle simulators, such as aircraft, tanks, and others, thanks to the PC, started to be sold commercially. This led to many other war-themed games to be released with help from defence companies collaborating with video game companies, such as Sega's collaboration with Lockheed Martin. Army simulators such as *Real War* released in September 2001 became available to the public. *Real War* was well received by the public after 9/11 because it allowed the public to "kill terrorists". Army training simulation games ordered by the Pentagon and developed by game company THQ, such as *Full Spectrum Warrior*, also started to be released commercially. Stahl investigates these games in order to find out how they aid in war and killing through social phenomena, such as collective condoning of state violence. New army recruitment strategies are used through video games as well. With the free release in 2005 of *America's Army*, which became far more popular in terms of exposure than expected by the military, the U.S. army had branched out from television and magazine ads into the realm of video games. The objective of this game was to enlist an additional 300 people per year into the U.S. military. In 2007, *America's Army* reached eight million registered users according to battle-tracker.com[3], and "forty percent of enlistees in 2005 had previously played the game" (Barnes quoted in Stahl, 2006, p. 123). As a result of the massive exposure this game has achieved, it has far surpassed its original objective as well as being one of the top tools creating "favorable awareness" for the military (Miller quoted in Stahl, 2006, p. 123). The blurring of the lines between citizen and soldier that video games create produces a "third sphere" of cultural production, in addition to the public and the private spheres, which is characteristic of social militarization (Stahl, 2006, p. 125).

By creating a friendly guise for the military, war video games strive to "[manufacture] consent and complicity amongst consumers for military programs, missions, and weapons, thus obfuscating the relationship between war consumers, institutions, and economies of violence" (Power, 2009, p. 209). It hopes to create an overall militarized home life where these "virtual soldier-citizens" can be trained. As Power (2009) argues "the U.S. military has invested millions of tax dollars in developing the game with a view to offering players the chance to virtually explore and 'experience' the Army from basic training all the way up to deployment and live situations that might be found in the global War on Terror, creating 'surrogate soldiers' along the way" (p. 203).

In closing I want to leave you with a quote from Sgt. Sinque Swales describing his experience in actual war events, which goes as follows:

> "It felt like I was in a big video game. It didn't even faze me shooting back. It was just natural instinct. Boom! Boom! Boom! Boom!... The insurgents were firing from the other side of the bridge... We called in a helicopter for an airstrike... I couldn't believe I was seeing this. It was like Halo. It didn't even seem real, but it was real". (Quoted in Vargas, 2006)

Conclusion

Through investigation and help from numerous researchers, the Pentagon's hold on the media becomes clearer to perceive. Through its efforts to control what is shown on screen, the Pentagon is able to create a positive message surrounding the military, keep war "clean" and sanitary, with no real images of violence and gore, turn war into a spectacle and blur the lines between citizen and soldier, and between reality and fiction. Through these methods America's imperialist efforts were able to create this shift towards militainment, in the hope of gaining support for its military campaigns through recruitment, strengthened hegemony, and normalized military action as a legitimate and just way of solving "world problems".

Militainment has many possible lasting effects on audiences that could be detrimental to populations locally and abroad. It has the potential to totally militarize the private and public spheres and eventually make the difference between citizen and soldier completely indistinguishable. Militainment reinforces attitudes of "let's Fight" as ways of solving problems and makes anyone who threatens Americans possible enemies that need to be killed for the greater good. War video games have a big part to play in the militarization of civilian life by actively engaging audience to participate in realistic war-like missions. The further technology advances, the higher the potential for war simulators and video games to become more and more realistic, making them better training and recruitment tools.

Notes

1   See Phil Strub's IMDB page, where the all the movies he has worked on can be found: http://www.imdb.com/name/nm0835243/

2   Laurie Adler's LinkedIn page: http://www.linkedin.com/pub/laurie-adler/5/582/361

3   See http://battletracker.com/forum/general/battletracker-news/163022-america-s-army-reaches-8-million-user-mark/ and for the number of recently active online players visit http://battletracker.com/index.php?page=AAOTrackerStats

References

Davidson, A. (2006). The "Soft" Power of Hollywood Militainment: The Case of the West Wings Attack on Antalya, Turkey. *New Political Science*, 28(4), 467–487.

Forte, M. C. (2008). Another Profile in Propaganda: Laurie Adler, U.S. Army's "Human Terrain System". *Zero Anthropology*, August 7. http://zeroanthropology.net/2008/08/07/another-profile-in-propaganda-laurie-adler-us-armys-human-terrain-system/

Harvey, D. (2003). *The New Imperialism*. Oxford, UK: Oxford University Press.

Hewitt, G. (n.d.). "Embedded" in Iraq. *BBC News*. http://news.bbc.co.uk/aboutbbcnews/hi/news_update/newsid_3850000/3850491.stm

Ignatius, D. (2010). The Dangers of Embedded Journalism, in War and Politics. *The Washington Post*, May 2.

http://www.washingtonpost.com/wp-dyn/content/article/2010/04/30/AR2010043001100.html

Omoera, O. S., & Ibagere, E. (2010). Revisiting Media Imperialism: A Review of the Nigerian Television Experience. *International Journal of Research & Review*, 5(1), 1–18.

Power, M. (2009). Digital War Games and Post 9/11 Geographies of Militarism. In R. Schubart, F. Virchow, D. White-Stanley, D., & T. Thomas (Eds.), *War Isn't Hell, It's Entertainment: Essays on Visual Media and the Representation of Conflict* (pp. 198–211). Jefferson, NC: McFarland & Company, Inc., Publishers.

Robb, D. (2004). *Operation Hollywood: How the Pentagon Shapes and Censors the Movies*. Amherst, NY: Prometheus Books.

Solomon, K. (2007). The Spectacle of War and the Specter of "The Horror": Apocalypse Now and American Imperialism. *Journal of Popular Film & Television*, 35(1), 22–31.

Stahl, R. (2006). Have You Played the War on Terror?. *Critical Studies in Media Communication*, 23(2), 112–130.

————— . (Writer and Producer). (2007). Militainment, Inc: militarism and pop culture [Documentary]. Northampton, MA: Media Education Foundation.

Takacs, S. (2012). *Terrorism TV: Popular Entertainment in Post-9/11 America*. Lawrence, KS: University Press of Kansas.

Thomas, T. (2009). Gender Management, Popular Culture, and the Military. In R. Schubart, F. Virchow, D. White-Stanley, & T. Thomas, T. (Eds.), *War Isn't Hell, It's Entertainment: Essays on Visual Media and the Representation of Conflict* (pp. 97–114). Jefferson, NC: McFarland & Company, Inc., Publishers.

Vargas, J. A. (2006). Virtual Reality Prepares Soldiers for Real War: Young Warriors Say Video Shooter Games Helped Hone Their Skills. *The Washington Post*, February 14.

http://www.washingtonpost.com/wp-dyn/content/article/2006/02/13/AR2006021302437_pf.html

Wells, M. (2003). Embedded Reporters "Sanitised" Iraq War. *The Guardian*, November 6.

http://www.theguardian.com/media/2003/nov/06/broadcasting.Iraqandthemedia

CHAPTER SEVEN

Defeating Disinformation: Hugo Chávez, the U.S., and Media as a Weapon

Gretchen Smith

Since 1998, the year Hugo Chávez assumed presidency, Chávez and the people of Venezuela have been a consistent target of U.S. imperialism. This fact has been repeatedly exemplified throughout the past decade through military and economic threats, diplomatic pressure, and the use of propaganda (Golinger, 2010). Throughout the presidency of George W. Bush (2001–2009), attempts to remove Chávez from office became blatant as the U.S. government openly identified him to the world as an international threat whose government opposed democracy. In reality, his story, his legacy, could not be any different. In his fourteen years of presidency, Hugo Chávez worked towards improving the lives of the impoverished within Venezuela and all of Latin America, as he led his Bolivarian movement forward. Social program funding skyrocketed with the nationalization of industries, illiteracy was eradicated, and heath care made free, creating a new Venezuela under an alternative model. Chávez's legacy was enormous, as he promoted the rights of women, the indigenous, and the impoverished, eliminating the barriers of racism and classism, and brought to the forefront the possibility and hope for actual change (Golinger, 2010). His Bolivarian movement influenced many within and outside of Venezuela, as he gave to those previously without one a voice and paved the path to an economic, political, and social alternative future.

Throughout this case study, I will analyze U.S. imperialist intervention within Venezuela since the first election of Hugo Chávez, with particular focus upon media coverage and its influence both in Venezuela and the U.S. Beginning with an overview of his movement, I will detail the Bolivarian revolution and the threat this alternative method poses to U.S. interests. I will then examine U.S. intervention in Venezuela through the coup d'état, the oil strike, and the referendum recall, showing Washington's actions to provoke regime change in Venezuela. Finally, I will focus upon the media both in the western hemisphere and particularly Venezuela, discussing the impact this media war has had upon public opinion and the effect of pouring millions of dollars into the media.

"¡Aló, Presidente!"

The Man and the Movement

The twenty years prior to Chávez taking office saw Venezuela in a drastic economic decline, with poverty rates soaring, political corruption constant, and repression profuse (Maduro, 2013). The people lacked trust in their government which lived off of the abundant oil wealth and favoured to the small elite, and as class divisions and frustrations intensified, the country went into a state of social and economic disorder. Venezuela was, needless to say, a country ready for revolution and in 1998, six years after his first unsuccessful attempt at revolt, Comandante Hugo Chávez was elected president of Venezuela and his Bolivarian Revolutionary Movement was underway. Evolving from the vision of Simon Bolivar, the early nineteenth-century liberator of Venezuela and other nations throughout Latin America from Spanish rule, the Bolivarian movement aims to transform Venezuela into a nation based on democratic socialism, breaking itself free from the imperial and hegemonic principles of the United States and western hemisphere (Gott, 2005). This revolution strived primarily to elevate the poor with the use of state resources and then reorienting domestic political structures, as it has produced a new constitution and new legislature, and to develop a foreign policy which unifies and strengthens Latin America and opposes neoliberal economic policies. Through promoting participatory democracy, the elimination of corruption, and equitable distribution of resources, Chávez developed a platform which has worked to improve democratic satisfaction among the masses along with the basic living standards for the majority of the poor in Venezuela. During Chávez's fourteen years of presidency, poverty was overall reduced by more than 50% and within a decade extreme poverty was shown to plummet from 25% to less than 7%, only some accomplishments among many others (Golinger, 2013).

Transforming Venezuela

Free education from preschool to doctoral studies has been made accessible to all and now that new schools have been built, and mobile education facilities established to tend to those living in less accessible areas, illiteracy has effectively been eradicated (Golinger, 2013). Free, universal healthcare has been introduced, providing doctors to regions which had previously seen none and sending the rates of infant mortality into decline (Golinger, 2013). Policies of participatory governance have been instated, which has placed power into community councils, giving a political voice to small rural areas formerly without one (Golinger, 2013). In effect, millions of Venezuelans' lives have drastically changed for the better and the social benefits of these changes have, to say the least, been profound and extensive as job creation, housing, land reform, and women's and Indigenous rights have all gained a strong focus with Chávez.

On the international level, the Bolivarian movement has worked towards building a unified Latin America through generating bilateral trade agreements along with social and economic integration, with presidents such as Evo Morales of Bolivia, Ignacio Lula da Silva of Brazil, Cristina Kirchner of Argentina, Fernando Lugo of Paraguay, and Rafael Correa of Ecuador, all of which began to follow and bolster the Bolivarian vision (Stone, 2009). With the creation of organizations such as the Bolivarian Alliance for the Peoples of Our America (ALBA), the Union of South American Nations (UNASUR), and the Community of Latin American and Caribbean States (CELAC), Chávez developed the incentive and possibility for the nations of Latin America to work together in terms of social, economic, and political co-operation (Maduro, 2013). Rising oil prices gave Venezuela the ability to share its wealth with others; throughout the past decade, billions of dollars have been distributed throughout the Americas (Weitzman, 2012, p. 104).

According to Columbia University and its "happiness survey," 84% of Venezuelans reported being "satisfied" with their lives, making it the most contented society in South America, and which aligns with several other international "happiness" survey such as the Gallup poll in 2011 which placed Venezuela as 5th worldwide (equal to Finland) out of 124 countries on the level of happiness its citizens reported, and ahead of many key western European states as well as allies of the U.S. in South America which the U.S. has praised as models of development, such as Colombia (Boothroyd, 2012). According to the Columbia University survey, wealth does not correlate so much with happiness, as does a perceived fairness in the distribution of wealth, thus Venezuela ranks so highly in the survey given that it is the most equal country in South America in terms of wealth distribution, and a glaring contrast to the U.S. Elias Eljuri, the President of Venezuela's National Statistics Institution, explained the likely cause of the outcome reported by the survey as being due to 13 years of social investment by the Venezuelan government, with about 61% of its total revenue in programs being aimed at citizen wellbeing; increased funding to all sectors of the country's education and health systems plus a variety of cultural and sports projects. This figure, he added, represents almost a 25% increase in social investment from previous governments, with the percentage of national revenue dedicated to social welfare between 1986 and 1998, the most recent pre-Chávez years, averaging 36.2% (Boothroyd, 2012).

As with any leader, any nation, Chávez and his governance had flaws, though given the statistics and level of life satisfaction found amongst Venezuelans, it would be misguided to argue that Venezuela would have been better off without him, that the world was unchanged by his actions, or that his accomplishments were outweighed by his failures. According to Washington however, Chávez's achievements, if mentioned, are presented as no more than political contrivances. Why?

Posing a Threat

Since taking office in February of 1999 the U.S. had kept a close eye on Chávez , though with George W. Bush the watch over Venezuela intensified and Washington's dissatisfaction with the progression of the nation was voiced, loudly and repeatedly. The U.S.

has traditionally shown hostility towards independent, nationalist governments of the world and Venezuela's introduction of an alternative model to that of the neoliberals sparked extreme concern and contempt from the western hemisphere as Chávez had "systematically dismantled the institutions of democracy and governance" (USEC, 2006). This is one of the main threats which Venezuela poses towards the U.S.: the Bolivarian movement with its shift towards a more balanced geopolitical structure and away from hegemonic policies, is a movement whose influence could extend well beyond its geographic location (James, 2006, 27). Chávez's resistance to the neoliberal economic, social, and political model has been one aspect contributing to the U.S.' disdain, though his re-nationalizing one of the biggest oil reserves on the globe was what possibly posed the most immediate threat perceived by Washington (Wilpert, 2007).

This change in oil politics along with the diminishment of U.S. influence and the further aggravation of anti-empire sentiment in Latin America in the wake of the U.S. war in Iraq, set the stage for the Bush administration to set in motion its imperialist agenda for Venezuela. In September of 2002 when Bush announced his National Security Strategy, declaring, "the right to resort to force to eliminate any perceived challenge to U.S. hegemony," this agenda was proven, as years of imperialistic intervention against Chávez and the people of Venezuela, featuring a coup, an oil strike, and electoral interference, had begun (Chomsky, 2003).

"Chávez, Amigo, el Pueblo está Contigo"

The Coup of 2002

The U.S. government supported and financed a military coup against Hugo Chávez which briefly, between April 11 and 13 of 2002, ousted the president, replacing him with their preferred figure, Pedro Carmona, the former head of the chamber of commerce (see Wilpert, 2003). To this day, Washington will deny having had any part in the coup that sought to overthrow Chávez, though documents obtained through the Freedom of Information Act prove that the U.S. funded opposition groups often fronting as NGOs along with political parties in attempt to unify the opposition in the months leading up to the election (Golinger, 2010). The cables, published by WikiLeaks, outline the objectives of the U.S. embassy which include "dividing Chavismo," "isolating Chávez internationally," and "protecting vital U.S. business" (USEC, 2006). Furthermore, the cables show millions of dollars being donated to hundreds of organizations and forums which sought to unite Chávez supporters and the opposition in hopes that opinions of the former could be swayed. The morning of April 11th showed supporters of the opposition marching the streets to the state-owned oil company, while at the presidential palace, pro-Chávez supporters demonstrated and voiced their solidarity with his government (Stone, 2009). The opposition, changing their route, marched to the palace to spark confrontation with the Chávistas and by the afternoon, confusion was nationwide due to false reports produced throughout the day by the privatize media stations such as RCTV (Stone, 2009). Military commanders in support of the opposition stormed the palace, demanding Chávez's resignation, kidnapping him and transferring him to an island for the days to follow as he offered himself, though he refused to resign his presidency (Stone, 2009). With Chávez in custody, Carmona was temporarily installed as the generals and other coup leaders celebrated inside the walls of the presidential palace, moving then to dismiss the Supreme Court and annul the Constitution (Golinger, 2006). In the U.S., the fabrications told by the private media in Venezuela were echoed, claiming Chávez was responsible for the deaths which had occurred in the clashes, and making clear their support for his overthrow (Stone, 2009).

The information was presented in a way which invariably created an image of Chávez that would instil fear and cause many to see him as no more than a tyrant, as they drove into the minds of viewers the idea that he was "evil" and a "slumlord" and attempted to link him to international terrorism (Golinger, 2010). Media in Venezuela, rather than displaying the counter-coup brought about by Chávez supporters and military personnel that had begun outside of the presidential palace, aired movies and cartoons to distract and sway Venezuelans from the political reality (Klein, 2003).

"Chávez, amigo, el pueblo está contigo," ("Chávez, friend, the people are with you") was shouted through Caracas as thousands of Chávistas went to the streets to demand the safe return of their democratically elected leader (Stone, 2009). This support, joined with the loyal part of the military in support of Chávez, was how Chávez's government reclaimed the presidential palace, temporarily reinstating the vice president until Chávez's return was guaranteed (Stone, 2009). Despite having reclaimed their territory, the private media stations, all of which were being shown throughout Venezuela, claimed that the chaos had ended and Carmona with his government were comfortably in power. In order to counter this false narrative, it was vital for Chávez's supporters to get Channel 8, the state owned station, up and running again (Stone, 2009). Once its signal had been restored, the fabrications of the private media were exposed and laid to rest, and calmness ensued, with constitutional authority being reinforced (Stone, 2009). Chávez's return to the palace on the 14th was greeted by a large mass of supporters and his speech, telling the nation to restore order and avoid the misinformation being fed to them, acted as an end to the days of drama and chaos brought about by the opposition and the forces supporting it.

This coup acted as one mission which sought to remove Chávez from power and was made possible by two key U.S. agencies, though there exist plenty of others, which provided the funding needed for the development of anti-Chávez, pro "democracy," political and social groups (Golinger, 2010). These agencies, including the U.S. Agency for International Development (USAID) and the National Endowment for Democracy (NED), worked together to sponsor those who organized, supported, and led the coup against Chávez (Golinger, 2010).

Each of these agencies came to Venezuela with a clear mission to fulfill Washington's goals of ousting Chávez (Golinger, 2010). USAID arrived to strip him of his power and facilitate the recall of the referendum, and NED to unite the opposition forces and strengthen its influence among the masses, as each since 2002 have had millions upon millions of dollars channelled through them from the State Department to organize and run the opposition and media campaigns which feed the national and international press with their preferred representations of reality (Golinger, 2011). Though these agencies were sent to "promote democracy" in Venezuela under the Bush Administration, the election of President Obama and the economic crisis which confronted the world in no way halted the imperialistic aggression or missions of USAID, and NED and their intentions have remained the same, "to counter the Chávez government" (Golinger, 2011b). In fact, the arrival of Obama would represent the first time a U.S., president has *openly* requested funding for anti-Chávez groups from the national budget, with $5 million allocated in the Foreign Operations Budget for 2012 (Golinger, 2011a). As Golinger (2011a) also reported, "just between the years 2008 to 2011, the US State Department channeled more than $40 million to the Venezuelan opposition, primarily directing those funds to electoral campaigns against President Chávez and propaganda slated to influence Venezuelan public opinion". The U.S. funding draws from the State Department's Economic Support Fund (ESF) and the USAID's interestingly-named Office of Transition Initiatives (OTI). As Golinger (2011c) later revealed, through the National Endowment for Democracy (NED), created by Congress and funded by the State Department, and the USAID, "Washington has channelled more than $100 million to anti-Chávez groups in Venezuela since 2002". A majority of those funds, Golinger found, "have been used to run opposition candidates' campaigns, as well as finance those well crafted media campaigns against the Chávez government that flood the national and international press". After the USAID-maintained offices in Caracas of the International Republican Institute (IRI), the National Democratic Institute (NDI), and Development Alternatives Inc. (DAI), were shut down with the passage of a 2010 law in Venezuela that prohibited foreign political funding, the U.S. Embassy's budget skyrocketed as if to make up for their absence (Golinger, 2011c). As Golinger (2011c) explains: "In 2010, the Embassy in Caracas had an annual budget of $18,022,000; in 2011 it dropped to $15,980,000. But in 2012, the budget swoops up to $24,056,000, nearly a $9 million increase". This happened even though the U.S. maintained no ambassador in Venezuela.

Along with Obama, Canadian Prime Minister Stephen Harper has also allocated funding to "promote democracy" in Venezuela. This funding began with the Mulroney government and directs assistance towards agencies fronting as NGOs throughout the Latin America, under an agency known as the Canadian Foundation for the Americas (FOCAL) which "is almost entirely dependent on government funding and is accountable to Parliament" (Fenton, 2009). These external agencies and this abundance of funding is what nurtures internal conflicts burdening Venezuela and serve as an important imperialistic tool for the U.S. in their aim to exploit and control the natural resources which come from Venezuela, ultimately seeking to shut down the anti-empire, pro-democratic ideals of Venezuela (Fenton, 2009).

"Striking" Oil

Following the coup d'état which had occurred just months earlier, Chávez was finally able to take control of the oil wealth coming from Petróleos de Venezuela (PDVSA), nationalizing it and beginning to redistribute its revenues to the people after having blocked its privatization and fought off an oil strike which economically severely damaged the country (Gott, 2005, p. 251). Prior to being elected, a small number of elite members of the society reaped the benefits of Venezuela's oil as profits were shown to be going only to the highest ranking employees and managers of the company rather than being directed to the nation as a whole (Gott, 2005, p. 135). With Chávez's policies clearly no longer favouring them and after the call of a "general strike" and worker lockout at the oil company in December of 2002, the wealthy took to the streets to join the opposition in their quest for regime change (Gott, 2005). This oil strike sought to economically sabotage Venezuela, a method which had previously been used by the U.S. and local middle-class opponents in Chile (1973) and Haiti (2004), in an attempt to oust Chávez and bring in a more "acceptable" government, one more aligned with Washington's ideals (James, 2006, p. 6). Following the coup, the U.S. increased funding to groups sponsored by the NED and USAID which not only worked directly with the opposition parties, but also with wealthy, privatized media companies such as Globovision, Venevision, RCTV, and Televen in an attempt to spread false and negative images of the president and provoke concern from the public (James, 2006, p. 8). Marches were numerous and clashes between middle- and upper-class opponents and Chávez supporters were almost daily in occurrence, though in the end, yet again, the opposition forces underestimated Chávez and the support he had generated from the lower classes as he was able to re-start and take control of the oil company by February of 2003 (Wilpert, 2007, p. 25). This swift recovery of the industry allowed for Chávez to pour funding into social programs in an act to meet the needs of the country's impoverished population, frustrating the opposition and their allies even more and by the following year yet another plan to oust Chávez was being put into full effect (Wilpert, 2007, p. 27).

The Recall Referendum

After having attempted to overthrow President Chávez through illegal means and measures, the U.S.-backed opposition decided to go about things a different way and take a legal approach, with the formulation of referendum petitions in an attempt to have his government recalled (Wilpert, 2007, p. 26). This plan of action began immediately following the oil strike and by December of 2003 they had collected 3.1 million signatures, 2.5 million of which were validated and used to summon the recall referendum (Wilpert, 2007, p. 28). Chávez won with 58% of the ballots, as the opposition and their noticeably weak leadership, led by Manuel Rosales, began to lose support from the middle classes and now lacked the power of the oil industry, the military, and the people, causing it to become less of a threat and more of an annoyance to the Chávez government (Golinger, 2006). This caused the opposition to finally and for the first time since his election recognize Chávez as the legitimate and democratically elected leader of Venezuela, and gave Chávez new confidence sending him into a new phase where his government would pursue "socialism of the 21st century".

The years followed showed a constant battle between Venezuela's government and U.S. sponsored propaganda, with every election, every move Chávez made, being attacked profusely. Though hopes were high that U.S.-Venezuelan relations would settle and ease with the election of Obama, the imperial measures continued and strategies regarding the "situation" in Venezuela were laid out (Kozloff, 2006). This can be exemplified through the analysis by CANVAS (Centre for Applied Non Violent Action and Strategies) in January of 2012, which was obtained through WikiLeaks and identifies the opposition's key stakeholders and their allies and a list of potential issues for their campaign (Kozloff, 2006). This document reveals the social, economic, international, and military concerns Washington has with Venezuela, as well as potential allies of the opposition's campaign (including student groups, political figures, foreign and independent media, etc.), and features a "list of issues with potential to be exploited throughout the campaign," showing that Obama's government and its interference measures have been and will be as relentless as Bush's was (Kozloff, 2006). This is further proven by Washington's most recent reactions to the election of Nicolás Maduro, as it refuses to recognize his 2013 electoral victory with 50.7% of ballots over Henrique Capriles' 49.1% (see Kovalik, 2013). Chávez and the people of Venezuela have been a consistent target of U.S. intervention; through intelligence, financial, political, and media channels, the U.S. has deliberately and obsessively acted to undermine and demonize Chávez and his government on both Venezuelan and

American soil in desperate attempts to reverse electoral results. Throughout the following section, I will demonstrate the imperialist measures taken by the U.S. through the usage of media as a weapon primarily throughout North America, gauging and discussing the international reaction to claims that Chávez was nothing but an anti-democratic despot, and I will discuss Washington's efforts to pummel the newly elected government of Nicolás Maduro.

Demonizing a Saint

Media in the U.S.

As Mark Weisbrot (2010) states, "on Venezuela, the media is like a jury of 12 with one brain". Throughout North America, the media have portrayed Chávez as a sinister, anti-democratic, autocrat, who is an international threat and danger to his people (Weisbrot, 2010). Starting with his election in 1998 and throughout every election he has democratically won since, the media have been relentless in demonizing Chávez and his government. Their distorted reports and slanted coverage have called for Chávez's elimination and global support for the US and their intervention as Fox News has repeatedly accused the Chávez government of terrorism, and the New York Times has claimed the South American nation is "more lethal than Iraq" (Golinger, 2010). His entire time in power, Chávez was ridiculed, and even through his illness and death, the media did not make an effort to hold their fire and instead continued to criticize his terms in power with the hope to sway the results in Washington's favour for the election held this past April, as in sickness and health, the media followed the same rule they had followed for years: "you can say almost anything you want about Venezuela, so long as it is bad" (Weisbrot, 2013).

To say the fabrications about Chávez and the amount of media attention he received was overtly and blatantly hostile and occurred far too often would be a gross understatement and this attention can no longer be deemed media coverage, but flat out propaganda working to further Washington's imperialist agenda. Such propaganda has been repeated by the major media corporations throughout the U.S., with Newsweek comparing Chávez to Hitler, Stalin, and Mussolini, CNN's David Frum depicting him as "a villain out of a batman movie: buffoonish and sinister in equal measure," and broadcaster Pat Robertson calling for his assassination as Venezuela was becoming "a launching pad for communist infiltration and Muslim extremism" (FAIR, 2013). Though the government before his was responsible for a massacre of some 3,000 people, the violence in Venezuela, as often believed by those outside the country, began with the election of Chávez. According to the media, this violence continued throughout Chávez's presidency, as the major media outlets have created a violent image for a man who, unlike Bush and Obama, never declared war upon nor waged acts of violence against other nations. Western media have been effective and have worked to further Washington's goals as they have convinced many, if not most, living outside of Venezuela that the nation is run by a greedy dictator, who profits from the oil wealth (Weisbrot, 2010). While propaganda has obviously been effective in western nations, the story in Venezuela is much different in that Washington's media war in some ways gave Chávez and his government electoral and political success throughout both Latin America and other nations developing alternatives to the neoliberal model. What then is the point of pouring millions of dollars into agencies that, rather than working to further imperialism, make anti-imperial sentiment even stronger?

Media in Venezuela

One of the Western media characterizations that gained a prominent place in international coverage, was that Chávez eliminated freedom of speech throughout Venezuela, as he shut down private television stations which he had deemed, "the four horsemen of the apocalypse" (Klein, 2003). These television stations were privately owned by elite members of Venezuelan society and partnered with U.S. brands such as Coca-Cola and Playboy, while they presented anti-Chávez programming around the clock (Klein, 2003). The closure of some of these television stations allowed for more balanced reporting and information access, and still both anti- and pro-Chávez stations can be accessed with ease throughout the nation, and no less than 94% of television that is viewed by Venezuelans is not pro-government and that five of seven major national newspapers are in support of the opposition (Carter Center, 2012, p. 3; Jones, 2013). In other words, while the majority of public media outlets are owned by the state, pro-Chávez coverage is not viewed by the majority of the people. When Chávez announced the end of RCTV's license, the mass media outlets in the U.S. saw another chance to attack and simplified the situation with CNN stating, "RCTV... is going to be shut down because President Hugo Chávez is not a big fan of it" (FAIR, 2013).

The media obviously played a significant, if not the most important role in the imperialist interventions which have been discussed, especially throughout the coup, oil strike, and election campaigns. During a time of economic decline, it is a wonder why Obama would increase funding to anti-Chávez groups as throughout the past decade it has not translated into any material results for the U.S. or its preferred Venezuelan political actors. Washington will remain hopeful that their funding eventually achieves the results they desire, that the leader they hand pick, perhaps even groom, will be the next leader of Venezuela, though with the most recent election results, their prospects are not looking good. Instead, it appears Chávez's legacy is alive and strong, and as Maduro takes the reins, the Bolivarian movement will continue to prosper, while Washington continues the attempt to rid the world of alternative government and economic models.

Maduro

The recent election of Nicolás Maduro, Chávez's successor, and the months leading up to it, showed the U.S. as relentless as ever. Immediately after the results of the election were released, the ploys to de-legitimize and defeat Maduro and his continuation of the Bolivarian revolution continued (Gowans, 2013). Obama's government requested a 100% recount of the vote, though this stance lacked support on the international stage. Secretary of State John Kerry went forward to announce the U.S. refusal to recognize the legitimacy of the democratically elected leader. Venezuela has been shown to have one of the most advanced polling systems in the world with next to no possibility of cheating the vote. The failure of the U.S. to recognize Maduro's success in the election has been another method in attempt to de-stabilize the government of Venezuela, as violence and clashes have been regular occurrences since the election as the U.S. "is not supporting democracy and stability in Venezuela; it is intentionally undermining it" (Kovalik, 2013). The imperialist measures taken by Washington will certainly continue and their funding of anti-Chávez along with anti-Bolivarian movement groups will persist as their imperialistic interest in to the oil wealth and alternative political and economic models taken by the government of Venezuela will progress.

As demonstrated, throughout the years Chávez was in presidency, the U.S. partook in intrusive measures in order to advance their imperialist agenda and further their military and political presence within Venezuela and Latin America as a whole. The media had a huge influence on the imperialist actions which were taken through the coup d'etat of 2002, the oil strike of 2003, and any electoral or political campaign since Chávez's first election. Chávez, a supporter of social benefits, improving education and health care, and favouring the advancement of the poverty stricken majority, was relentlessly demonized by the organizations funded and sponsored by Washington and its agenda. Chávez's legacy was enormous, as he promoted the rights of women, the indigenous, and the impoverished, eliminating the barriers of racism and classism and brought to the forefront the possibility and hope for change. His Bolivarian movement influenced many within and outside of Venezuela, as he paved the path to an economic, political, and social alternative future. As Eva Golinger writes, he was "a maker of dreams for millions around the world" (Golinger, 2013).

Of particular interest in this investigation of the relationship between society and the environment is how an agenda of environmental conservation has been used by the West to pressure developing nations into conforming to international policies which have affected their national development. This has interfered with developing nation-states' sovereignty and self-governance. This form of manipulation, which can be viewed as a technique to maintain the hierarchical order between nation-states, and between the rich elites and poor peasants of all nations, is termed Eco-Imperialism.

References

Boothroyd, Rachael. (2012). Venezuela Happiest Country in South America. *Venezuela Analysis*, June 10.

http://venezuelanalysis.com/news/7044

Carter Center. (2012). Carter Center Study Mission Pre-Election Report for the Oct. 7, 2012, Venezuelan Presidential Election. *The Carter Center*, October 5.

http://www.cartercenter.org/resources/pdfs/news/peace_publications/election_reports/venezuela-pre-election-rpt-oct-2012.pdf

Chomsky, Noam. (2003). *Hegemony or Survival: America's Quest for Global Dominance*. New York: Metropolitan Books.

Fenton, Anthony. (2009). The Revolution Will Not Be Destabilized: Canada's "Democracy Promotion" in Venezuela. *Venezuela Analysis*, April 7.

http://venezuelanalysis.com/analysis/4356

Golinger, Eva. (2006). *The Chávez Code: Cracking US Intervention in Venezuela*. Northampton, MA.: Olive Branch Press.

——————. (2010). U.S. Buys the Press in Venezuela. *Z Magazine*, September.

http://www.zcommunications.org/u-s-buys-the-press-in-venezuela-by-eva-golinger.html

——————. (2011a). Obama Requests Funding For Venezuelan Opposition in 2012 Budget. *Postcards from the Revolution*, February 17.

http://www.chavezcode.com/2011/02/obama-requests-funding-for-venezuelan.html

——————. (2011b). Washington Plans Further Actions Against Venezuela. *Z Net*, June 9.

http://www.zcommunications.org/washington-plans-further-actions-against-venezuela-by-eva-golinger.html

——————. (2011c). US: $20 Million for the Venezuelan Opposition in 2012. *Venezuela Analysis*, August 12.

http://venezuelanalysis.com/analysis/6418

——————. (2013). Hugo Chávez, Dream Maker. *Z Net*, March 7.

http://www.zcommunications.org/hugo-Chávez-dream-maker-by-eva-golinger.html

Gott, Richard. (2005). *Hugo Chávez and the Bolivarian Revolution*. London, UK: Verso.

Gowans, Steven. (2013). Chávez's Enemies Hand him his Greatest Tribute: Defamation. *What's Left*, March 7.

http://gowans.wordpress.com/2013/03/07/chavezs-enemies-hand-him-his-greatest-tribute-defamation/

James, Deborah. (2006). U.S. Intervention in Venezuela: A Clear and Present Danger—Strategies and Tactics Used by the U.S. Government to Undermine Democracy, Sovereignty, and Social Progress in Venezuela During the Chávez Era–And What U.S. Citizens Can Do to Stop It. *Global Exchange*, January, 1-38.

http://www.globalexchange.org/sites/default/files/USVZrelations1.pdf

Jones, Owen. (2013). Hugo Chavez was a Democrat, not a Dictator, and Showed a Progressive Alternative to Neo-Liberalism is both Possible and Popular. *The Independent*, March 6.

http://www.independent.co.uk/voices/comment/hugo-chavez-was-a-democrat-not-a-dictator-and-showed-a-progressive-alternative-to-neoliberalism-is-both-possible-and-popular-8522329.html

Klein, Naomi. (2003). Venezuela's Media Coup. *The Nation*, February 13.

http://www.thenation.com/article/venezuelas-media-coup#

Kovalik, Dan. (2013). U.S Must Recognize Venezuela's Elections.

Huffington Post, April 18.

http://www.huffingtonpost.com/dan-kovalik/us-must-recognize-venezuela_b_3103540.html

Kozloff, Nikolas. (2006). *Hugo Chávez: Oil, Politics and the Challenge to the United States*. New York: Palgrave Macmillan.

Maduro, Nicolás. (2013). Under My Presidency, Chávez's Revolution Will Continue. *The Guardian*, April 13.

http://www.theguardian.com/commentisfree/2013/apr/12/my-presidency-Chávez-revolution-continue

FAIR. (2013). In Death as in Life, Chávez Target of Media Scorn. *Fairness and Accuracy in Reporting (FAIR)*, March 6.

http://fair.org/take-action/media-advisories/in-death-as-in-life-chavez-target-of-media-scorn/

Stone, Oliver. (Director). (2009). *South of the Border* [Documentary]. Canoga Park, CA: Cinema Libre Studio.

USEC. (2006). USAID/OTI Programmatic Support for Country Team 5 Point Strategy. U.S. Embassy-Caracas, diplomatic cable, ID: 06CARACAS3356.

http://www.cablegatesearch.net/cable.php?id=06CARACAS3356&version=1314919461

Weisbrot, Mark. (2010). Misreporting Venezuela's Economy. *The Guardian*, September 11.

http://www.theguardian.com/commentisfree/cifamerica/2010/sep/10/venezuela-economics

————— . (2013). Media Hate Fest For Venezuela Keeps On Keepin' On. *Al Jazeera English*, January 30.

http://www.aljazeera.com/indepth/opinion/2013/01/201312912275351687.html

Weitzman, Hal. (2012). *Latin Lessons: How South America Stopped Listening to the United States and Started Prospering*. Hoboken, NJ: John Wiley & Sons, Inc.

Wilpert, Gregory (Ed.). (2003). *Coup against Chavez in Venezuela: The Best International Reports of What Really Happened in April 2002*. Caracas: Fundación por un Mundo Multipolar y Fundación Venezolana para la Justicia Global.

Wilpert, Gregory. (2007). *Changing Venezuela by Taking Power: The History and Policies of the Chávez Government*. London, UK: Verso.

CHAPTER EIGHT

Eco-Imperialism

H. Jordane Struck

C ulture shapes how people understand their environment and how they act towards it. Nature (the environment) and society are in a constant state of co-production, a sort of symbiotic relationship in which the environment changes with cultural shifts and people are culturally influenced by their environment and how they perceive it. In many cases a society's historical interaction and understanding of their environment can have profound effects on their present environmental practices (Roos & Hunt, 2010). Even a single environment can be viewed in very different ways by peoples of different societies because of their cultural norms, values and practices which have been constructed through historical, economical, political and spiritual forces (among many others). For pastoralists and foraging native and indigenous groups the environment holds a quite different meaning from that of a western industrialized bureaucrat. The symbolic value of the land, which is culturally imbued, shapes the way society views and acts towards the land (Jay & Morad, 2002).

Of particular interest in this investigation of the relationship between society and the environment is how an agenda of environmental conservation has been used by the West to pressure developing nations into conforming to international policies which have affected their national development. This has interfered with developing nation-states' sovereignty and self-governance. This form of manipulation, which can be viewed as a technique to maintain the hierarchical order between nation-states, and between the rich elites and poor peasants of all nations, is termed Eco-Imperialism.

Defining Eco-Imperialism

There are many ways to view nature in relation to humanity, all of which are socially constructed and have their roots in a long history of interaction with the environment. At one time, nature was viewed as something to be colonized by humanity, there to be the resource cache for human development and survival (Roos & Hunt, 2010). This view is intrinsically imperialist and it is one of the foundations of eco-imperialism. The view of nature as something that is to serve the needs of humanity is maintained yet modified in eco-imperialism: nature is now further as serving the needs of Western nation-states exclusively and not those of the developing world.

"Under the guise of 'climate change' and 'resource protection' the developed North seeks to control, both physically and practically, the resources of the less developed world" (Soomin & Shirley, 2009, p. 846), and they do this by using the latest technologies and science to argue that developing nations must conform to strict environmental codes which ultimately limit their growth and ability to effectively raise their standard of living. There have even been efforts in the United Nations Security Council, led by the U.S., to have "climate change" declared a "peace and security issue" (see Black, 2011). The West is arguably trying simultaneously to hold the developing world back while advancing and protecting their own interests concerning the environment; attempting to maintain what parts of the environment are still sustainable and dictate who may use the resources and who may not, even outside of their own borders. This means that although the West contributes to 60% of carbon emissions, they politically and economically pressure countries such as Brazil not to exploit the resource-rich Amazon rainforest by arguing that it is necessary for reducing carbon emissions and for the survival of the planet (Soomin & Shirley, 2009). In a Marxist vein, this could be conceived of as a universally equal law which maintains universal inequality.

Environmentalism's increasing importance has been due to a number of changes in the dominant understandings of the environment. The way the environment is socially constructed is based on a society's understanding of nature (science), views on beauty (aesthetics), and observation (empirical) (Balasubramaniam, 1998,

p. 389). With new scientific research on the effects of pollution such as greenhouse gases, climate change and melting polar ice-caps, this knowledge has become more prominent in the media. Western societies have undergone a cultural change in that many now view "saving" the environment as their prerogative. As many in Western society have become more disillusioned with the material achievements of capitalism, modernization and development, environmentalism has also become a political subject of great concern and has changed the way the peoples and states, both developed and underdeveloped, view and act towards the environment today (Balasubramaniam, 1998).

The imperialist agenda has now moved away from controlling territories to preserving foreign resources for future consumption (Soomin & Shirley, 2009). It is inevitable that the developed world will require the developing world's resources once their own have been depleted (which is happening at an ever increasing rate). These resources will be used to benefit the future generations of the developed world instead of helping the impoverished and hungry people of the contemporary world. The developed world has already enjoyed a century of plentiful resources and fossil fuels which they exploited from lands which were not theirs and now they wish to further maintain control over the resources outside of their borders (Soomin & Shirley, 2009). This results in the West attempting to curtail the use of pesticides in Third World agricultural practices, pesticides which may eradicate malaria as it once did in their countries, because it is now viewed as environmentally harmful (Driessen, 2004). Also, many of the products which are grown in poorer countries are exported to the West for consumption even though pesticide use may be regulated and/or illegal in the importing nations, which only underscores the hypocrisy of Western political stances towards environmental practices.

Eco-imperialism is a Western political practice that attempts to overrule the sovereignty and self-governance of developing nation-states. Developing nations have little power in the international community and the more developed nations dictate the terms of environmental use and protection, through tariffs, fines, trade embargoes and corrupting political leaders. Therefore, "the interpretation of environmental imperialism thus hinges on a contrast between 'environmentality' and 'governmentality'" (Dyer, 2011, p. 187). Some, such as Dyer (2011), view eco-imperialism as both a cause for imperialism, because it limits the freedoms and rights of less powerful nations, and also as an unusual and ambiguous form of imperialism, because it represents a large group of diverse views and imperatives. Dyer (2011) states that new environmental policy is emerging from a shifting understanding of the environment and that it represents global trends, and not just those in the West, and that at the worst this represents a "participatory empire". Participation here is not meant to mask continuing inequalities in the distribution of wealth and resources.

The rhetoric of eco-imperialism can be deployed in many ways: it can be focused on development, self-governance and/or indigenous rights. Eco-imperialism has become contested terrain in global and local politics and those involved often view the issues in divergent ways. It can be seen as an imperative stemming from the "top-down" or from the "bottom-up" (Dyer, 2011). What this means is that there is an environmental agenda which exists both for the developed world and for those in the developing world. Local indigenous populations have fought to protect their territories and the environment in which they live, seeking assistance in the global community and from international regulating bodies, such as the United Nations (UN). Conversely developed nations have tried to implement international environmental regulatory policies which infringe on the territories and sovereignty of less developed nations. So it is the case that environmentalism can be both a source of hegemony as well as one of resistance (Dyer, 2011). The major difference is that in the case of resistance, sovereignty is contested within domestic borders and does not impinge on other foreign states. The agreement of the state to protect the environment of its indigenous population is far different from the imposition of environmental policy on one state by another. The idea that environmentalism can be seen both as a source for maintaining empire and also one for combating it is very interesting and shows how a single event or single political issue can be interpreted and presented in multiple ways which may contradict each other, yet nonetheless coexist.

It can also be argued that developing nation-states are forced to exploit their own indigenous peoples' lands due to economic pressure in the world market created by developed nation-states and that this is a form of coerced eco-imperialism, arguably a form of self-colonization. All of this hinges on the reality that capitalism constantly requires new markets and resources to promote growth and that the world economy is inherently capitalist.

The capitalist world economy also creates a system of ecological unequal exchange, in which more developed and higher-consuming countries redirect portions of their environmental costs to lower income countries, which in turn increases environmental degradation in the latter, while lowering levels of resource consumption in the former (Jorgenson, 2009). This shows how, using Wallerstein's world systems paradigm, it can be argued that just like commodities, ecological resources flow towards the core away from the periphery nations and create economic and social disparity (Nash, 1981; Harvey, 2003). These unidirectional flows of natural resources accelerated between 1975 and 2000 and the exchanges between developed countries and underdeveloped countries have only become more unequal (Jorgenson, 2009). Although nation-states may have undergone significant political and economic changes during the last three decades, little has changed in regard to the environmental burden which is being laid on underdeveloped nations. The developed world is content to maintain the status quo, in which it maintains a dominant position.

Unequal Environmental Exchange

The unequal exchange of ecological resources is also directly tied to a nation's ecological footprint, which is the measured ecological degradation created by a nation's consumption and development. This also accounts for multiple variables such as imported/exported resources and waste management. According to Jorgenson (2009), using the Global Footprint Network (2006), the per-capita footprint of lower-income countries is far below the average footprint size of all nations and the per-capita footprint size of high-income countries is well above the average. In short, people in developing nations are surviving on far less than the average individual requires, and people in developed worlds are consuming far more than they require. This is due to many social and cultural factors, but is maintained through global dominance, in which developing nation-states are criticized for exploiting their own natural resources to better their own people's material existence and lift them out of poverty and despair, while the West expands with impunity. Unfortunately, at times the local elites of lower-income countries, who are corrupted or are in partnership with higher-income countries, decide to sell off their countries' resources at a cost of environmental malpractice; at other times it is the chain of control of transnational corporations which influences the flow of natural resources to richer countries.

This form of environmental cost shifting can also lead to the "Netherlands Fallacy" which refers to the assumption that the overall environmental impact of the Netherlands is contained within its national borders (Jorgenson, 2009). This would make it appear as though more developed nations are practicing lower re-source consumption and contributing less to pollution than may be the case. More developed nation-states have little trouble with eco-logical degradation as long as it is to their benefit and is not hap-pening within their borders, and sometimes they consider degradation within their borders excusable, as long as the stakes are high enough and profits are assured.

Oil

Oil in many ways fuels the world economy: it feeds, shelters and clothes us, as it is a basic ingredient in a huge number of products; and it is used in the production of an even larger number of prod-ucts (Wood, 2006). Oil fueled the food production revolution and the war machines of the last century (Canty, 2011; Harvey, 2003). In essence, war was also the reason oil became the fuel of choice for the industrialized world. It was during the end of the nine-teenth-century that oil was urged upon the British Navy as being a better energy source than coal and one that would keep them in control of the waters. The British government invested in private companies to secure foreign oil sources so as to supply the mili-tary's demand (Shaffer, 2006). Seeing the importance of oil in World War I, the U.S. followed this trend. U.S. president Woodrow Wilson even received a letter from French president Georges Clemenceau which stated that oil was "as necessary as blood" (quoted in Shaffer, 2006, p. 57). The only difference between the British and American systems was that rather than create incen-tives for a few chosen companies, they decided to support a multi-plicity of companies searching to secure oil in foreign markets. Today, the U.S. uses far more oil than it produces and its military expenditures outweigh those of every other country's military ex-penditures combined (Harvey, 2003). The U.S. is the largest eco-nomic power in the world and it is also the largest user of oil. This oil is largely found in foreign reserves, an aspect which compounds the disparities in international levels of development. The U.S. only has enough oil reserves within its borders to last a possible 11 years, while Canada has potentially enough oil to last 15 (a calcu-lation which does not include the Alberta tar sands) (Shaffer,

2006). If the more optimistic appraisals of the amount of reserve oil in the Alberta tar sands are correct, then Canada is home to the largest, or second largest, oil reserves in the world and this makes it a political, economic and military target for the U.S. (Shaffer, 2006).

The U.S. has taken a vested interest in the tar sands and has pushed U.S. oil companies to make aggressive and large investments in these sources. Through acquiring the stock of Canadian oil companies such as Imperial Oil and Petro Canada, U.S. companies have been able to secure a strong hold on Canadian oil and this can have serious implications. Canada has the potential to either use this oil for their own economic benefit, or to sell it to competing nation-states, but at the moment 90% of exported Canadian oil and 100% of its exported natural gases are sent to the U.S.; 24% of U.S. oil is imported from Canada and this number is speculated to rise significantly by 2030 (Government of Canada, 2013).

Canadian and U.S. governments have shared a long history of mutual cooperation, but there have been pacts and agreements made, especially within the framework International Energy Agency (IEA), which have been disadvantageous to Canadian interests. The problem is that voting power is not evenly distributed and though Canada is the largest oil-producing nation of the G-7, the country has only four percent of the voting rights, while the U.S. has 26% and even Japan has 10% (Shaffer, 2006). The U.S., therefore, is the largest consumer of oil in the world, has the most political and economic control of it and the U.S. military is the single largest consumer of oil in the U.S. That military is then used, when it is deemed necessary, to secure oil reserves in foreign lands. This cyclical process shows how the control of oil reinforces the international system in which developed countries maintain a hegemonic control over less powerful countries and preserve the status quo. Because Canada has so little say in the use of its oil in the IEA and because the U.S. uses almost half of its oil to power its war machine (Wood, 2006), Canada therefore may be inadvertently fueling wars in foreign lands which it both ideologically and politically does not support, yet in which it is economically implicated nonetheless (Shaffer, 2006). The Canadian Government must make strategic decisions about how to handle their potentially enormous oil reserves because whether or not the government decides to continue a laissez-faire economic policy, it will significantly change the dynamics of international relationships. Recently, the government of Conservative Prime Minister Stephen

Harper removed protection from the majority of waterways within Canada, allowing for development in these places and facilitating the building of pipelines such as that proposed by Keystone XL. The U.S. may be very optimistic about these developments because it will supply them with readily available oil much more efficiently, but there have been many concerns raised by Canadians and even attempts to destroy the pipeline using less than legal means so the Canadian government may yet change course and take firmer control of these vast resources.

In short, the U.S. has taken many precautions to maintain their control on a long-term oil source and it is fueling their international supremacy as the world's sole superpower. As Senator Henri Bélanger said in during World War I, "He who owns the oil owns the world... Who has oil has empire" (quoted in Shaffer, 2006, p. 54).

Water

The issue of the sustainability of water and its central importance in the survival of all living organisms situates it as a subject of great importance and demands serious attention. Currently, of the world's more than 7.1 billion inhabitants, more than 1.3 billion are without adequate drinking water and two-thirds may be subject to serious "water distress" by 2025. Globally, 70% of water is used for agricultural production, showing how water is inextricably connected to food production and sustainability (FAO, 2013; UN Water, 2013; UNESCO, 2012; World Water Council, 2013). That there would be a relationship between water and empire should not come with much surprise.

The role agribusiness plays in the equation is discussed later, but it is no coincidence that water supplies and services within the U.S. are being continually privatized. Once again this means that quality and supply will be dictated by profit margins instead of by human need and demand (Bozzo, 2008). In terms of quality, and in relation to the previous section on oil, we should note that the production of a barrel of oil creates four barrels of polluted, toxic and permanently unusable water (Bozzo, 2008). Canada is also home to 70% of the world's fresh water supplies, which once again shows how Canada will be a site of central importance in the future of the geopolitics of the environment.

Western states also blatantly overlook and disregard the protests and appeals of other nations concerning development around waterways and push ahead with industrial development regardless of the resistance of these other nations. A prime example of this occurred when an Esmeralda mining operation accidentally spilled hazardous chemicals into the Tisza River and this flowed downstream into the Danube and eventually the Black Sea causing serious environmental damage (Harper, 2005). There had been protests against this mining operation for years, but to no avail: Esmeralda was able to reach an agreement with the Romanian government and got the operation underway even though there were serious environmental concerns. Ultimately, the chemical spill killed 1,240 metric tons of fish and polluted the water downstream so badly it was unsafe for use (Harper, 2005). This aggravates the fact that already 120 million in Europe do not have access to safe drinking water (UNESCO, 2012, p. 9). The Esmeralda incident shows how both borders and sovereignty were transgressed and how these actions had implications wider than just for the nation which supported the mining company and was home to the operation. All parts of our environment are intricately intertwined without any regard to nation-state borders; the actions taken by one country will certainly affect nations in their proximity and probably those further away.

The deregulation and privatization of water, and the pollution of water caused by oil production, will be of great importance in future political discussions and are of central importance when discussing the new imperialism. For the West to continue producing oil, it must both pollute water and at the same time preserve sufficient amounts for future consumption. This means polluting foreign waters and preserving domestic drinking supply. This will have the effect of denying other peoples their right to water, eventually killing them, in spite of the fact that water is considered a human right by the UN (see UNDESA, 2013).[1]

Food Production

Another issue of great importance when investigating eco-imperialism is the role food production has taken in this globalized hegemonic system. There are three points that need to be made about food production and how it has been used to systematically disadvantage the poor while supporting the rich elites of the world. First, food production in many cases has historically been undertaken by the colonized of the empire and this practice has not changed in the post-colonial context due to the ability of the international capitalist market to sustain long-term unequal exchange. The process of colonized peoples producing goods as slaves has been replaced by a system which coerces peoples in those same regions where slavery predominated, and other "formerly" colonized territories, through market forces and also through the use of interventions or coups orchestrated by the U.S. and the Central Intelligence Agency (CIA) (Harvey, 2003)—as, for example, in the case of the CIA's overthrow of Jacobo Arbenz Guzman in Guatemala in 1954, to protect the interests of the United Fruit Company (see Kinzer & Schlesinger, 2005). Such interventionist tactics have been used many times in Central and South America (Faber, 1993). The main products which were being produced by these countries to be exported to the U.S. were coffee, cotton, sugar and bananas. Most of these crops were grown for export and were controlled by U.S.-owned companies who operated these foreign agribusinesses. The safety levels were minimal and so was the pay to the labourers who toiled in these jobs. The economic benefits which were afforded the Central American states were minute and were essentially enjoyed only by a very small group of powerful elites and did nor reach the poor (Faber, 1993). Political leaderships in these states were corrupted and sold out their lands and peoples for a chance to be like the elites of the Western world, or were summarily replaced through U.S. intervention (Harvey, 2003).

Second, the consequences of the control of food production by the U.S. in foreign markets not only led to environmental degradation and social inequality, but also displaced local farmers from their land, forced them onto lands which were unfit for agricultural use and led to a lack of food for locals, severely affecting the local economy and drastically elevating poverty levels (Faber, 1993). In Nicaragua and Guatemala, thousands of peasants who resisted eviction were killed during U.S.-supported counterinsurgency operations during the 1960s through the 1980s (Faber, 1993, p. 50). In Central America many wildlife habitats, the rainforest and other important ecological lands have been cleared to make way for pastures and other agricultural projects. Virtually all coastal savannas and evergreen forests have been destroyed as well to court the economic potential of urban bourgeoisie and landed oligarchs (Faber, 1993).

Third, it is not just that the U.S. and other developed nation-states are interfering and controlling the food production in foreign markets for their own personal benefit, but also that they are curtailing food production within their own borders (Kenner, 2008).

Corporations such as Monsanto which have strong ties to the federal and state governments within the U.S. use these connections to buy control of the U.S. food market. By supporting political leaders and their parties, big agribusiness has been able to create a near monopoly on the food industry within the U.S. This has also been fueled by advances in agricultural technology with the use of combustion engines which have allowed a farmer to go from producing enough food for 11 people to producing enough for 160 people (Canty, 2011). Small farms that want to produce food on a small local scale are harassed by federal agents and put to stringent tests which in many cases shut them down (Canty, 2011). The food which is produced by the much larger agribusiness corporations is standardized and contains many preservatives and other chemicals which allow it to be produced in such an industrial way. The food produced by small operation farms does not conform to the codes which these large companies coerce/ convince/ bribe/ corrupt federal bodies to pass.

One particularly unfortunate story is that of a sheep farm in Pennsylvania which had its livestock seized and put to death illegally due to pressure from a competing agribusiness farm. The animals were treated inhumanely, killed and dumped in a local garbage depot because they were diagnosed by the Food and Drug Administration (FDA) with a disease which does not even exist for sheep: Mad Cow Disease (Canty, 2011). There are other very serious cases such as Monsanto's proposed bill to enforce the use of Genetically Modified Organism (GMO) corn and wheat strains within the U.S., but these decisions have not yet been reached.

Food production and consumption in the U.S. is a virtual monopoly of big agribusiness like Monsanto and standardized in a way which ensures the greatest possible profits, while overlooking issues of nutrition, health, animal rights and the destruction of the environment. The way that food is produced in big agribusiness is premised on the idea that altering food will have no effect on the environment, so companies manipulate genes, confine livestock, change diets, use corn to feed everything and change the very way we as a society understand food culturally. It also takes large amounts of oil to grow and transport food the way it is presently distributed, which undermines local growing economies and puts increased pressure on the dependence on oil. The effect of allowing these companies free rein will be an exclusive reliance upon their services for sustenance.

Recently Hungary has decided to no longer do business with Monsanto or to use their products (they have destroyed all Monsanto GMO fields) and so have many other countries that once went through the imperial process described above and are attempting to take back control of their national self-determination and sovereignty (True Activist, 2012). Hopefully these few large companies will never control all the systems of food production in the world, but stopping them will take a concerted effort by many peoples. For the moment Western states are content signing over their subsistence requirements to large capitalist corporations.

Native Americans

The systematic injustices inflicted upon Native Americans during the colonial period continue today, and though they have changed form in many ways they merely extend the socially devalued position which Native groups were assigned during the height of their oppression. Native Americans were forced onto reserves and now those lands are being polluted by the U.S. government and by private companies that are looking to dispose of their toxic wastes. This has been termed "environmental racism" or even "environmental genocide" (Brook, 1998) and epitomizes the continued subordinate role Native Americans play in their relationship with the state. Some bands and tribes have agreed to the building of facilities on their lands in an effort to overcome economic disparity and because no other sources of income are available to them. There are also individual Natives who make illegal agreements with companies who wish to dump on Native lands, while some companies simply abuse Native lands by dumping without prior consent (Brook, 1998).

In a survey of 25 American Indian reservations, it was revealed that 2,500 hazardous waste generators and other hazardous waste activity was taking place in close proximity to their borders (Brook, 1998). The U.S. is placing these dangerous sites with no regard for the concentration of the population of Native groups close to them. Toxic waste pollution can lead to a plethora of health problems which can be extremely hard on peoples who have little in the way of economic means to seek help in hospitals in which adequate care may not be afforded them due to institutionalized racism.

There are also many claims by First Nations communities in Canada that their health is being severely affected by the oil ex-

traction taking place in the Alberta tar sands. There has been serious speculation that the chemicals which are flowing downstream are leading to higher levels of cancer within these
communities along the Athabasca River. So it can be seen that the
value being placed on oil by the U.S. and Canada, and the necessity of obtaining oil by any means to run an army, are indirectly
contributing to the ecological degradation of Indigenous lands and
their peoples. To compound these egregious assaults, Indigenous
lands are regularly threatened by the pollution which emanates
from uranium and coal mining, and the fall-out from weapons test-
ing and spent ammunition shells from the U.S. military (Brook,
1998). All of these assaults are reprehensible, not only because
they are all environmentally damaging acts, but also because they
undermine Indigenous sovereignty (Brook, 1998). This form of domestic eco-imperialism is also a cultural violation because many
Indigenous Peoples' histories and traditions are embedded within
the environment in which they have lived for many generations.

The United Nations

Recently the United Nations (UN) has been criticized for its
agenda for international environmental policies which they discussed at Rio+20. These complaints have come from both the political "right" and the political "left" (Newman, 2012). The main
concern on both sides has been that the UN is trying to implement
international laws to further structure the way countries act towards their environment and nature—acting, in short, as a form of
ecological world police. Those on the right believe that the policies
curtail economic possibilities for investment and growth, that they
would significantly affect an economy which is already faltering
and that they are a way of implementing a "global socialist authority" (Newman, 2012). Those on the left, as well as Indigenous
communities, argue that what is really happening is that the rich
countries of the world are trying to implement measures to secure
resources in poor countries for their own future use. Vandana
Shiva, a well-known Indian activist, reportedly said that, "this
whole green economy thing, interpreted as a planetary grab of the
remaining resources, is not going to solve anything" and she concluded saying that, "the real agenda is privatizing the planet... For
the one percent, as the occupy movement called it" (Newman,
2012).

The Rio+20 summit shows, according to critics, how global power elites can come together to dictate the way the entire world interacts with the environment while simultaneously transgressing national sovereignty, and peoples' freedom and prosperity (Newman, 2012). Though some may mistakenly view the UN's environmental agenda as something that is being used simply to slow down economic growth and that it is a form of socialist "eco-terrorism" which is trying to abolish capitalism and instill communist values (Poole, 2011), the truth is that many extremely poor nations have millions of citizens who are starving and do not have access to drinking water, shelter and sometimes even clothing, that not allowing these nations to avail themselves of the means to meet the needs of their dying citizens is the real problem with the UN's policies on the environment (Driessen, 2004). People who live in rich countries have problems which, though they may be serious, are usually far less grave than those of people in poor countries. It may seem overly relativistic, but to impose the same laws of environmental development on all nations will lead to the same inequalities being reproduced. Marx had the same objection to the laws of the state being administered equally to all because they thereby ignored the salient economic inequality which existed in society. Marx's objection can very easily be transposed onto environmental laws and policies, especially considering how important natural resources are to the growth and development of the economy. By creating environmental laws which apply to all nations equally, the UN will not only undoubtedly reproduce the economic inequalities which presently exist, but also maintain a disproportionate allocation of resources for future consumption by the West which already uses far more resources than are needed. By maintaining a market which is the exclusive domain of the world elite, the UN is allowing the capitalist economy to continue until all available resources are consumed—the only possible result of a never-ending expanding market within a environmental system with finite energy and resource limits.

Conclusion

The West's view of the environment as a source of potential economic profit and resource for human consumption is a culturally constructed ideology. It is not an ideology shared by all societies in the world, but due to the transnational growth of the capitalist economic system, this ideological view of the environment has predominated globally. Whether it has been adopted or resisted, it has had undeniable effects upon other areas of social, political and economic importance. In a world in which the global economy encourages environmental depredation and high levels of material consumption it is difficult for nations, especially underdeveloped nations, to practice environmental conservation and sustainability. Many developing nation-states are forced to exploit their environment to extract their only valuable resources. At the same time they are being chastised by the developed nations of the West for undertaking environmentally unfriendly practices in order to achieve similar standards of living. The West, having reached an elevated standard of living, does not need to exploit its environment as much as it once did, so it can now afford to preach sustainability to peoples whose cultures it has disrupted and often whose economies it has left in tatters. Now that the West has begun to realize an ecological agenda, it is upset that the rest of the world, still reeling from the effects of primary contact, is trying to gain economic independence and maintain sovereignty. This is a double standard. The West needs to ease its oppression and support the poorer nations in a search for some measure of equality. Without considerable accommodation on both sides, there is little chance that developing nations will have the ability to reach levels of adequate standards of living without causing some forms of irreversible environmental degradation.

At the moment, the rich nations are merely continuing the process of "ecological colonialism" which is described as the process by which Europeans systematically replaced Indigenous ecosystems with European agricultural ecology throughout the colonial period (Jay & Morad, 2002). Just as imperialism has been viewed as displaced but continuing with the new empire of the U.S., so the spread of environmental ideology and practices has continued to spread and invade the diverse peoples and cultures of the world. The U.S., through collusion with other developed nations, and with complete disregard for less powerful nations, is enforcing an agenda in which it maintains its supremacy over all others through the control and regulation of natural resources, as well as the flow of dangerous and toxic materials. The system enriches the rich while endangering or killing those on the periphery. The economic growth depends on the devaluation and/or destruction of other markets (Harvey, 2003); the prosperity of one environment is premised on the destruction of other environments. Unfortunately, ecosystems are intrinsically linked, and pollution can only be compartmentalized and displaced for so long before it eventually corrodes the entire system.

Notes

1   For example: On July 28, 2010, through Resolution 64/292, "the United Nations General Assembly explicitly recognized the human right to water and sanitation and acknowledged that clean drinking water and sanitation are essential to the realisation of all human rights. The Resolution calls upon States and international organisations to provide financial resources, help capacity-building and technology transfer to help countries, in particular developing countries, to provide safe, clean, accessible and affordable drinking water and sanitation for all". In November 2002, the Committee on Economic, Social and Cultural Rights adopted General Comment No. 15 on the right to water. Article I.1 states that "The human right to water is indispensable for leading a life in human dignity. It is a prerequisite for the realization of other human rights". Comment No. 15 also defined the right to water as "the right of everyone to sufficient, safe, acceptable and physically accessible and affordable water for personal and domestic uses". Source: UNDESA, International Decade for Action, "Water for Life," 2005-2015 at http://www.un.org/waterforlifedecade/human_right_to_water.shtml. See also UNGA (2010), ECOSOC (2002), and a list of additional international covenants recognizing the right to water as a human right as found here: http://en.wikipedia.org/wiki/Right_to_water#Right_to_water_in_inter national_law.

References

Balasubramaniam, V. (1998). Environment and Human Rights: A New Form of Imperialism. *Economic and Political Weekly*, 33(8), 389–390.

Black, T. (2011). The Rise of the Eco-Imperialists: Why the United Nations is Wrong to Depict Everything from War and Famine as a "Climate Change Issue". *Spiked Online*, July 25.

http://www.spiked-online.com/site/article/10919/

Bozzo, S. (Director). (2008). *Blue Gold: World Water Wars* [Documentary]. Irvine, CA: Purple Turtle Films.

Brook, D. (1998). Environmental Genocide: Native Americans and Toxic Waste. *American Journal of Economics and Sociology,* 57(1), 105–113.

Government of Canada. (2013). Canada and the United States: Energy Relations.

http://can-am.gc.ca/relations/energy-energie.aspx?lang=eng

Canty, K. (Director). (2011) *Farmegeddon: The Unseen War on American Family Farms* [Documentary]. Warren, NJ: Passion River Films.

Driessen, P. (2004). The West's Eco-Imperialism against the Third World. *House of Representatives Subcommittee on Energy and Mineral Resources*, February 4 [Video].

http://www.youtube.com/watch?v=L9oN2mOkA5w

Dyer, H. (2011). Eco-Imperialism: Governance, Resistance, Hierarchy. *Journal of International Relations and Development*, 14, 186–212.

ECOSOC. (2002). Substantive Issues Arising in the Implementation of the International Covenant on Economic, Social and Cultural Rights, General Comment No. 15: The right to water. United Nations Economic and Social Council, Committee on Economic, Social and Cultural Rights.

http://www.unhchr.ch/tbs/doc.nsf/0/a5458d1d1bbd713fc1256cc400389 e94/$FILE/G0340229.pdf

Faber, D. J. (1993). *Environment under Fire: Imperialism and the Ecological Crisis in Central America*. New York: Monthly Review Press.

FAO. (2013). FAO Water—Topics: Water Scarcity. United Nations Food and Agriculture Organization.

http://www.fao.org/nr/water/topics_scarcity.html

Harper, K. (2009). "Wild Capitalism" and "Ecocolonialism": A Tale of Two Rivers. *American Anthropologist*, 107(2), 221–233.

Harvey, D. (2003) *The New Imperialism*. New York: Oxford University Press.

Jay, M., & Morad, M. (2002). Cultural Outlooks and the Global Quest for Sustainable Environmental Management. *Geography*, 87(4), 331–335.

Jorgenson, A. K. (2009). The Sociology of Unequal Exchange in Ecological Context: A Panel Study of Lower-Income Countries, 1975–2000. *Sociological Forum*, 24(1), 22–46.

Kenner, R. (Director). (2008). *Food Inc.* [Documentary] New York: Magnolia Pictures, Participant Media, River Road Entertainment.

Kinzer, S., & Schlesinger, S. (2005). *Bitter Fruit: The Story of the American Coup in Guatemala*. 2nd ed. Cambridge, MA: Harvard University Press.

Nash, J. (1981). Ethnographic Aspects of the World Capitalist System. *Annual Review of Anthropology*, 10, 393–423.

Newman, A. (2012). The Real Agenda Behind UN "Sustainability" Unmasked. *The New American*, July 9.

http://www.thenewamerican.com/rio-20/item/12008-the-real-agenda-behind-un-%E2%80%9Csustainability%E2%80%9D-unmasked

Poole, D. (2011). The U.N. and the Eco-Terrorist Plot to Abolish Capitalism. *The Examiner*, July 10.

http://www.examiner.com/article/the-u-n-and-the-eco-terrorist-plot-to-abolish-capitalism

Roos, B., & Hunt, A. (Eds.). (2010). *Postcolonial Green: Environmental Politics and World Narratives*. Charlottesville, VA: University of

Virginia Press.

Shaffer, E. H. (2006). Canada's Oil and Imperialism. *International Journal of Political Economy*, 35(2), 54–71.

Soomin, L., & Shirley, S. (2009). Eco-Imperialism: The Global North's Weapon of Mass Intervention. *Journal of Alternative Perspectives in the Social Sciences*, 1 (3), 846–860.

True Activist. (2012) Hungary Destroys All Monsanto GMO Corn Fields. *True Activist*, February 10.

http://www.trueactivist.com/hungary-destroys-all-monsanto-gmo-corn-fields/

UNDESA. (2013). International Decade for Action, "Water for Life," 2005-2014. United Nations Department of Economic and Social Affairs.

http://www.un.org/waterforlifedecade/human_right_to_water.shtml

UNESCO. (2012). Managing Water under Uncertainty and Risk. United Nations World Water Development Report 4. United Nations World Water Assessment Programme/United Nations Educational, Scientific and Cultural Organization.

http://unesdoc.unesco.org/images/0021/002154/215492e.pdf

UNGA. (2010). Resolution adopted by the General Assembly, 64/292. The human right to water and sanitation. United Nations General Assembly, 64th Session, Agenda item 48, August 3.

http://www.un.org/ga/search/view_doc.asp?symbol=A/RES/64/292

UN Water. (2013). UN Water Statistics: Water Resources. UN Water.

http://www.unwater.org/statistics_res.html

Wood, J. J. (Director). (2006). *Crude Impact* [Documentary]. Sausalito, CA: Vista Clara Films.

World Water Council. (2013). Frequently Asked Questions.

http://www.worldwatercouncil.org/programs/right-to-water/faq/

CHAPTER NINE

A Discussion of Debates and Potential Limitations of Ethical Critiques of the Human Terrain System

Nathaniel Millington

Whether it is ethical to use anthropological expertise in the interest of state security has been a fruitful ground of debate between anthropologists and academics. In 2007, the fire of this debate was fanned when the U.S. Army introduced the Human Terrain System (HTS), a military branch that made use of experts from different social science disciplines in order to provide a cultural advantage in the military's counter-insurgency (COIN) efforts. Because of their historical involvement and subsequent disillusionment with the military, anthropologists have been especially vocal in their critique of the HTS. While the usage of anthropological data as means of securing a strategic military advantage is not unprecedented, the recent development of the HTS has renewed discussions concerning the ethicality of a public association between the social sciences and the U.S. military. The purpose of this paper is firstly to briefly trace the political conditions that paved the way for the introduction of the HTS as well as the arguments of those for the ethical involvement of anthropologists in military operations. After reviewing the academic reaction to the implementation of the HTS, this paper will then look at the ways in which critiques of HTS on the grounds of professional ethics may be limited. Finally, it will show that, even if a strong case is made for the ethical use of anthropological expertise to reduce the human cost of war, it is undermined by the mismanagement of

the HTS and its ultimate failure to reach its goal of reducing kinetic violence in COIN operations.

American Imperialism and the Inception of HTS

The American invasion of Afghanistan and Iraq in 2003 has put to
rest many questions about American imperialism. While the U.S.
government touted that their intervention in the region was motivated by a humanitarian spirit of wanting to establish peaceful
democracies, those critical of the Bush administration argued that
the true intentions of the world hegemon were of an imperialistic
nature; in seeking to establish western friendly democracies in
Iraq and Afghanistan, the true desires of the U.S. were to protect
and extend their geo-political and economic interests throughout
the world (Daily, 2010). The events in the following years, however, have proven to be strategically difficult for U.S. military operations in the region. Despite the U.S. overthrow of the Taliban
regime in Afghanistan and the U.S.' proclaimed victory over Saddam's Ba'athist government in Iraq, the U.S.-led coalition remained on shaky ground and quickly lost control of both countries.
What followed was a notable increase in violence between different
groups, paving the way for an emergence of insurgencies. Some-
time between 2005 and 2006 elements within the U.S. army began
to put together the Human Terrain System to further advance
their political and strategic goals, which signalled a significant
shift in U.S. military strategy—from conquering the geophysical
terrain to conquering the human terrain, described as "the social,
ethnographic, cultural, economic, and political elements of the
people among whom a force is operating...defined and characterized by sociocultural, anthropologic, and ethnographic data" (Kipp
et al., 2006, pp. 9, 15).

The shift of focus to the "human terrain" reflected a novel
change in U.S military strategy in the Middle East. In September
of 2006, Bush elected to review his administration's failing policy
in light of the significant increase of violence in the region. Cementing this change in policy was the replacement of General
George Casey by General David Petraeus as Commander of Multi-
National Forces-Iraq in February of 2007. The change toward a
"more culturally sensitive military" was accompanied by the subsequent military "surge" into Iraq by the end of 2007, introducing
at least 20,000 more soldiers into the area (Greenstone, 2007).
This shift in policy is also reminiscent of the (Robert) Gates Doc-

trine, which called for a stronger relationship between the military and education institutions (Hill, 2009). Gates argues against the monolithic idea of security agencies whose function is solely to uniformly follow orders and advocates that the "new" military should embrace the world's ideological and intellectual climate (Hill, 2009).

The Birth of HTS

HTS represented the culmination of the efforts by political and military leaders to produce a more "culturally sensitive" war. Instrumental in the creation of the HTS was Montgomery McFate, a cultural anthropologist, who strongly advocated for anthropological engagement in military affairs between "asymmetric adversaries". In her work on what she termed "the military utility of understanding adversary culture," McFate pointed to the historic relationship between cultural knowledge and warfare and argued that anthropology was developed "largely to support the military enterprise" (2005b, p. 47). In the same work she continues to cite examples of the synergistic relationship between anthropology and the military throughout the first and second world wars, the Vietnam War, and several proxy wars. According to her, that anthropology is the handmaiden to colonialism is common wisdom—and a tradition to live up to. Examples to support this claim include the use of Ruth Benedict's 1946 study on Japanese culture in the *Chrysanthemum and the Sword* and Ladislas Farago's work, *German Psychological Warfare*, to gain cultural understanding of adversary culture during World War II (McFate, 2005a). McFate cautions that the absence of anthropology from the public arena (read: military) can lead to rendering the discipline "exotic and useless," borrowing the words of A. L. Kroeber. McFate calls for an adaptation of this relationship to suit the asymmetric relationship that characterizes the situation in Afghanistan and Iraq. More specifically, she argues for cultural sensitivity to the relatively new phenomenon of insurgency, characterized in the U.S. military field manual as an "organized movement aimed at the overthrow of a constituted government through use of subversion and armed conflict," in a, "protracted politico-military struggle designed to weaken government control and legitimacy while increasing insurgent control" (McFate, 2005a, p. 25). She warns that regardless of the anthropology community's reluctance to participate in warfare, cultural information on adversary culture is becoming increasingly valuable to the Department of Defense (DOD) (McFate, 2005b). The result of the absence of participation by anthropologists can be the use of incomplete or bad cultural information which can in turn lead to failed operations and policies, meaning more possible casualties, be they Americans, insurgents, or civilians, (McFate, 2005a).

The transition to the "culturally sensitive war" in the Middle East, a transition from idea to policy, began in 2005 when McFate and Andrea Jackson submitted a pilot proposal to the Pentagon Office of Operational Cultural Knowledge which called for a focus on the human terrain and an implementation of social scientists in combat operations (González, 2008). The final product was the HTS program, which was to send out five-person Human Terrain Teams (HTT) to evaluate and provide reports of the human terrain. According to McFate, this evaluation consisted of exploiting "the underlying tribal structure of the country; the power wielded by traditional authority figures; the use of Islam as a political ideology; the competing interests of the Shia, the Sunni, and the Kurds; the psychological effects of totalitarianism; and the divide between urban and rural" (McFate, 2005b, p. 37). The purported success of HTS has been widely controversial; some have claimed it to have effectively reduced kinetic (violent) operations in the region (McFate, 2005a; Greenstone, 2007; Daily, 2010) while others have dismissed these statements as mere fluff, lacking evidence to support them, while also pointing to the ethical pitfalls of anthropological involvement in the military (American Anthropological Association [AAA], 2007; Commission on the Engagement of Anthropology and U.S. Security and Intelligence Communities [CEAUSSIC], 2009; González, 2008; Price, 2009a).

Figure 9.1: "Key Leader Meeting"

A Human Terrain Team consisting of U.S. Army soldiers and civilians, along with an Afghan interpreter, conduct a key leader meeting with the village elder of Koshab Village, Afghanistan, April 3 [2011]. (Photograph: U.S. Central Command [CENTCOM]).

Academic Reaction

The anthropological community has been the most vocal group among scholars in general in their criticism of HTS. As previously mentioned, the relationship between anthropology and the military has had a tumultuous past characterized by shifting relationships of collaboration and rejection. The professional code of ethics of anthropology, and U.S. military interventions abroad, seem to have somewhat of a symbiotic relationship. The American Anthropological Association established its first ethical code in 1971 following the Vietnam War (Fluehr-Lobban, 2008). In contrast with some other codes of professional ethics such as those established as a result of the Nuremburg trials, the ethical code outlined by the AAA imposes no legal accountability on members of the anthropological community. However, it is a good indication of the ethical opinions held by many anthropologists who participate and subscribe to the AAA. In the ethical code developed in response to the Vietnam War, which formally "delinked" anthropology from the military, the rules suggested that all research should be open and transparent, that the individuals being studied are able to opt out of the research at their own discretion, and that anthropologists should be held accountable to their research communities and must be certain that no harm would come to them as a result of their research, directly or indirectly (Mountcastle & Armstrong, 2010, p. 161).

The participation of anthropologists in HTS once again confronted the AAA with the question of re-assessing the ethical nature of the engagement of the discipline with the military. In October of 2007, the AAA's executive board issued an official statement on the HTS program, publicly condemning it on the grounds that it violated the established ethical code that was written in blood as a result of anthropologists' prior engagements with the military. The ethical concerns outlined by the AAA pointed to the trouble of gaining proper informed consent in the context of war and the difficulties anthropologists engaged with the military may have in fulfilling the tenet of doing no harm to the individuals they study

The condemnation of HTS by the AAA gathered further support amongst notable organizations in the anthropological community. The Association's Commission on the Engagement of Anthropology with the U.S. Security and Intelligence communities (CEAUSSIC) concluded in 2009 that, "when ethnographic investigation is determined by military missions, not subject to external review, where data collection occurs in the context of war, integrated into the goals of counterinsurgency, [...] it can no longer be considered a legitimate professional exercise of anthropology". (CEAUSSIC, 2009)

Additionally, in the summer of 2007 the Network of Concerned Anthropologists (NCA) was founded in response to the Pentagon's policy of hiring social scientists for military work (Jackson, 2008). One goal of the NCA is to monitor activities related to the role of anthropologists in the military, for example the funding of research, the expectations of that research, and its impact on the discipline. Finally in this short list of academic reactions, in 2010 six of the nine living ex presidents of the AAA, 37 chairs of anthropology, and 40 anthropology department chairs (including those of Harvard University, Stanford University, and University of Chicago) signed a petition urging Congress to stop funding HTS (Albro & Gusterson, 2012).

The Seductiveness of HTS and Neo-Realism

In her work on HTS and the "seduction of ethics," Maja Zehfuss attempts to shed light on the limitations of the anthropologists' critique derived from professional ethics. As of April 2009, there were only 11 social scientists that possessed a degree in anthropology (masters or PhD) out of the total 417 social scientists employed by HTS at the time (Zehfuss, 2012, p. 178). The danger, then, in proposing a critique in terms of professional ethics designated for a particular subgroup of social science is that it enables that critique to be compartmentalized (Zehfuss, 2012). She does acknowledge that it is appropriate for anthropologists to consider their position on the issue based on the concerns of their discipline, but maintains that this focus on the anthropological code allows for the conclusion that HTS should hire other social scientists from other disciplines (Zehfuss, 2012). However, whether this conclusion is arrived at or not, Zehfuss shows that, during its formative years, HTS suspiciously avoided the oversight of an Institutional Review Board which would have provided a discipline neutral review of the ethicality of the program.

In the same vein, Zehfuss argues that it is both problematic and futile to make a distinction between professional ethics and politics. Doing so could make the professional code of ethics an "extra-political" standard which limits the ethical critique of HTS as it makes it difficult to critique such an "ethico-political" project in the framework of the supposed political neutrality of ethics (Zehfuss, 2012, p. 186). Zehfuss then points out the seductive appeal of HTS has that is often overlooked by those critical of the program and shows that it may be troublesome, given the constraints of *ethical* reasoning, to condemn those who participate in HTS if they have no malevolent intentions (2012, p. 183). It is important to consider the "seductiveness of the expectation that cultural expertise can contribute to making war less destructive" (Zehfuss, 2012, p. 183). Eric Daily makes a similar point when he advocates for a "short-term morality," in which he prioritizes the immediate preservation of Iraqi and Afghan lives over any anti-imperial sentiments (2010, p. 6). Daily specifies that if the program did nothing to help the lives of the local populations and only used cultural knowledge to help targeting, his support for the program would be retracted. However, many critics have suggested that this seduction may be an illusion created by the way in which HTS has been packaged as a "kinder, gentler counterinsurgency" which so far has been completely unsupported by evidence (Zehfuss 2012, p. 183). Nevertheless, this seductiveness lends credence to Zehfuss' caution against separating professional ethics from politics.

The positions taken by those defending HTS seem to have in common the recognition that U.S. imperial activities in the Middle East will continue to happen despite condemnation by the intellectual (anthropological) community. This sentiment is reminiscent of neo-realist theory of international relations. This theory assumes the international system to be anarchic (Waltz, 1988) and thus perennially dangerous and loaded with violent conflict. While this may not be entirely true due to the degree of authority exercised by international institutions, nonetheless the hegemon of the system, the U.S., has been known to ignore this authority in order to advance its own interests on many occasions in the past—the most recent being the invasion of Iraq in 2003 and Afghanistan in 2001. Neo-realists place extraordinary emphasis on the quest for "power" as the motivation of actors within the international system, virtually naturalizing the pursuit by states to secure and extend geopolitical and economic interests as a permanent and normal fact of global relationships (Waltz, 1988). In looking at the question of ethics from a neorealist perspective, which is what I believe underlies the McFate's approach, this allows us to better understand

McFate's warning against what she sees as the *isolationist* tendencies of the anthropological community that push anthropologists to retreat into their "ivory tower" (McFate, 2005a, p. 28). Not quite an anti-intellectualist position, this is an argument for the integration of the intellectual community with the "public sphere" (narrowed to mean the state, and more specifically, the military and intelligence apparatuses)—the search then is for a fusion of anthropological professional ethics with "real world" politics. Thus one possible option, undertaken by some of those anthropologists engaged in HTS, is a shift from the tenet of "do no harm" to "lessening harm" (Fluehr-Lobban, 2008, p. 19).

One problem with looking at this issue from a neo-realist perspective is that doing so may undermine or disempower efforts of decolonization which have been a main concern of the anthropological community (particularly within the AAA) in the post Vietnam War intellectual climate. On the other hand, however, neo-realist theory allows for the assumption that in some cases (especially where the hegemon is involved) these efforts of decolonization are futile in the anarchic international system where states will use their (seemingly limitless) military power to pursue their own ends. Thus, neo-realist thought will at most allow for the potential of lessening harm to humans by acknowledging the inevitably violent nature of the international structure.

What Really Happened With HTS

The anthropological community has not only been critical of the way in which HTS conflicts with the professional ethics established by the AAA. The other arena of discussion is related to the actual way in which HTS has unfolded on the ground in Iraq and Afghanistan. Many U.S. media publications and articles from military journals have touted the success of HTS in reducing kinetic operations. Very critical of this success was Roberto González who has been a key debater against HTS within the AAA. As previously mentioned, González claims that anthropologists who are enchanted with the idea of HTS as a kinder, gentler insurgency are fooled by the way HTS has been packaged. The results that point to this gentler insurgency are dubious at best. When he questioned the claim that one HTT helped reduce violence in Afghanistan by 60%, anthropologist David Price discovered that there was no such evidence (2009b). Other journalists have also demanded evidence pertaining to the reduction of kinetic operations in the region to no avail (Weinberger, 2008). Journalist John Stanton also published a series of investigative reports that revealed "widespread financial mismanagement, lack of accountability and programmatic conditions indicative of a military-contract-without-accountability gone wild" (Price, 2009a). Moreover, in an article written to boast of the "catastrophic success" of the HTS, McFate showed that the program absorbed $150 million per year from the taxpayer funded U.S. defence budget (McFate, 2011). When taken together, the sheer expensiveness of this mismanaged program along with the lack of evidence for any of its claimed success strengthens the claim that HTS is packaged as a gentler counterinsurgency merely to gain public support for the neo-colonial presence of the U.S. in the Middle East (Price, 2009b). One result of this gross mismanagement of HTS may be the discrediting of possibly valid points concerning the ethical involvement of anthropology, the value of cultural knowledge in military operations, while hindering the chance of adapting the professional ethical code to account for real-world politics in order to lessen harm in an imperialistic setting. In "All Our Eggs in a Broken Basket," Major Ben Connable expands on this idea and shows that the HTS approach ignores "recent improvements in military cultural abilities" (2009, p. 57). Finally, the fact that the U.S. government opted to develop and publicise HTS in favour of taking advantage of the cultural abilities of combat veterans previously embedded in the field lends further credence to González's earlier point that HTS is a political strategy to gather public support.

Conclusion

A critical evaluation of HTS reveals that there is little or no evidence to support the claims that it has reduced kinetic violence in Iraq and Afghanistan. From the U.S. military's perspective, however, HTS may appropriately be considered a success (if we agree with González's opinion) precisely by attracting the attention of numerous uncritical U.S. media publications, thus giving it a "free ride" into the hearts and minds of the U.S. population and many social scientists who participated in the program (Price 2009b). However, does the failure of HTS negate some anthropologists' views that it may be ethically unacceptable to actively engage in military operations? Here the obstacles that HTS runs up against HTS include both arguments that it conflicts with professional ethics, and condemnations of its insidious political design. The answer for HTS supporters is that there is value in anthropological engagement with the military on the grounds of a "short term morality," in order to lessen the harm done to the victims of an imperialistic nation. However, for that argument to succeed there must first be a critical examination of the military culture that produces HTS. John Allison's experience as a "double agent" in the HTS training program at Fort Leavenworth provides a good example of the need to study the effects of the U.S. military industrial complex. After an attempt to help bring positive change to the HTS from the inside, Allison observed that the HTS is designed to "harden [trainees] to the fact that warfare is primarily kinetic violence; to prepare them to subordinate their goals to the goals of the kinetic missions of the fighting force, and to see the Afghan or Iraqi people as needing US-Style education including values indoctrination and moral/ethical training" (Allison, 2010). In another section of his "Leavenworth Diaries," Allison notes that the U.S. military industrial complex is analogous to a "computer virus that is introduced into the basic program of the nation" (Allison, 2010).

If there is any weight to the aforementioned arguments, such as those for the involvement of anthropologists in the military and the merging of anthropological ethics with politics, they could only be conceivable in a military climate that had been cured of this "computer virus". To complicate things, it could be that these imperialistic tendencies cannot even be separated from this virus. However, to use the language of George R. Lucas, to even begin considering the ethical use of anthropology "for" the military, there must be continued research on anthropology "of" the military as a cultural institution (2008).

References

American Anthropological Association (AAA). (2007). American Anthropological Association's Executive Board Statement on the Human Terrain System Project. American Anthropological Association. November 6.
http://www.aaanet.org/pdf/EB_Resolution_110807.pdf.

Albro, R., & Gusterson, H. (2012). Commentary: 'Do No Harm'. *Defense News*, April 25.
http://www.defensenews.com/article/20120425/C4ISR02/304250001/Commentary-8216-Do-No-Harm-8217-

Allison, J. (2010). The Leavenworth Diary: Double Agent Anthropologist inside the Human Terrain System. *Zero Anthropology*, December 5.
http://zeroanthropology.net/2010/12/05/the-leavenworth-diary-double-

agent-anthropologist-inside-the-human-terrain-system/

Commission on the Engagement of Anthropology with the U.S. Security and Intelligence Communities (CEAUSSIC). (2009). Final Report on The Army's Human Terrain System Proof of Concept Program. October 14.

http://www.aaanet.org/cmtes/commissions/CEAUSSIC/upload/CEAU SSIC_HTS_Final_Report.pdf

Connable, B. (2009). All Our Eggs in a Broken Basket: How the Human TerrainSystem is Undermining Sustainable Military Cultural Competence. *Military Review, 89*(2), 57–64.

http://www.au.af.mil/au/awc/awcgate/milreview/connable_mar09.pdf

Daily, E. (2010). Escorted Ethnography: Ethics, the Human Terrain System an American Anthropology in Conflict. *Berkeley Undergraduate Journal*, 22(2), 1–31.

http://escholarship.org/uc/item/2021q00k.pdf

Fluehr-Lobban, C. (2008). Anthropology and Ethics in America's Declining Imperial Age. *Anthropology Today*, 24(4), 18–22.

González, R. J. (2008). "Human Terrain": Past, Present and Future Applications. *Anthropology Today*, 24(1), 21–26.

Greenstone, M. (2007). Is the 'Surge' Working? Some New Facts. Massachusetts Institute of Technology, Department of Economics, Working Paper Series, Paper 07-24, September 18.

http://ssrn.com/abstract=1014427

Hill, M. (2009). "Terrorists Are Human Beings": Mapping the U.S. Army's "Human Terrain Systems" Program. *Differences: A Journal Of Feminist Cultural Studies*, 20(2/3), 250–278.

Jackson, J. E. (2008). Anthropologists Express Concern over Government Plan to Support Military-Related Research. *MIT Faculty Newsletter*, 20(5), May/June.

http://web.mit.edu/fnl/volume/205/jackson.html

Kipp, J.; Grau, L.; Prinslow, K,; & Smith, D. (2006). The Human Terrain System: A CORDS for the 21st Century. *Military Review*, September-October, 8–15.

http://usacac.army.mil/CAC2/MilitaryReview/Archives/English/Milita ryReview_20061031_art005.pdf

Lucas, G. R. (2008). The Morality of "Military Anthropology". *Journal Of Military Ethics*, 7(3),165–185.

McFate, M. (2005a). Anthropology and Counterinsurgency: The Strange Story of Their Curious Relationship. *Military Review*, March–April, 24–38.

http://www.au.af.mil/au/awc/awcgate/milreview/mcfate.pdf

——————— . (2005b). The Military Utility of Understanding Adversary Culture. *Joint Forces Quarterly*, (38), 42–48.

http://www.au.af.mil/au/awc/awcgate/jfq/1038.pdf

——————— . (2011). Reflections on the Human Terrain System during the First 4 years. *Prism*, 2(4), 63–82.

http://www.ndu.edu/press/reflections-human-terrain-system.html

Mountcastle, A., & Armstrong, J. (2010). Obama's War and Anthropology: Ethical Issues and Militarizing Anthropology. *Social Justice*, 37(2/3), 160–174.

Price, D. H. (2009a). Counterinsurgency, Anthropology and Disciplinary Complicity. *CounterPunch*, February 3.

http://www.counterpunch.org/2009/02/03/counterinsurgency-anthropology-and-disciplinary-complicity/

————— . (2009b). Counterinsurgency's Free Ride: The Press and Human Terrain Systems. *CounterPunch*, April 7.

http://www.counterpunch.org/2009/04/07/counterinsurgency-s-free-ride/

Waltz, K. N. (1988). The Origins of War in Neorealist Theory. *The Journal of Interdisciplinary History*, 18(4), 615–628.

Weinberger, S. (2008) The Pentagon's Culture Wars. *Nature*, 455(2), 583–585.

Zehfuss, M. (2012). Culturally Sensitive War? The Human Terrain System and the Seduction of Ethics. *Security Dialogue*, 43(3), 175–190.

CHAPTER TEN

Anthropology against Empire: Demilitarizing the Discipline in North America

Maximilian C. Forte

"When the university turns away from its central purpose and makes itself an appendage to the Government, concerning itself with techniques rather than purposes, with expedients rather than ideas, dispensing conventional orthodoxy rather than new ideas, it is not only failing to meet its responsibilities to students; it is betraying a public trust".—J. William Fulbright (1967, p. 1555)

Just as during the Vietnam war, when Senator J. William Fulbright wrote the words in the opening quotation, the last decade has been marked by the increased militarization of relations between the U.S. (and its closest allies) and the rest of the world. The tragic result has been a far too easy and rapid resort to military intervention, often as an option of first resort. In this context, private defense contractors consume ever larger portions of national budgets, a result of the wider military corporatism that dictates national priorities. Newer ideologies of intervention ("humanitarianism," "protection," and "democracy promotion"), and even older narratives of conquest (defending "the civilized world"), have become normalized. "Counterinsurgency," a favoured doctrine from the Vietnam War years, has been rehabilitated (for a while). Seen in this light, it is very important that anthropologists such as Hugh Gusterson (2007) have issued a challenge in calling for an anthropology that is more cognizant of how militarism often shapes both our own research topics and "field sites". He argues that militarism ought to be a subject of theoretical and empirical inquiry as much as colonialism or post-colonialism have been. I would add that the proper focus should be imperialism, the system that conceives and nourishes contemporary militarism.

By way of extending the emerging anthropology of militarism, I begin this chapter by first discussing the call for anthropology of militarism. I do so in order to broaden the call to one that focuses on North American militarism within the historical context and analytical framework of imperialism. In addition, I engage in this discussion in order to bring the focus back to the militarist tendencies within anthropology.

This leads to the second stage, dealing with the militarization of contemporary anthropology in North America, as part of a broader process that involves repositioning academic anthropology as an imperialist discipline (once more). I will thus review some of the key efforts to re-imperialize anthropology, especially in light of the U.S. "war on terror" and various so-called "humanitarian interventions" in which Canada has actively participated, and in which there has been a marked "cultural turn" (Gregory, 2008). Recruiting anthropologists in order to acquire "ethnographic intelligence" (Renzi, 2006), map social networks, and search for culturally viable means of "winning hearts and minds," are key elements of the shift to "population-centric" counterinsurgency. Surveillance, pacification, and dominance are thus its most obvious goals. For anthropologists, the most prominent example of this pursuit has been embodied by the U.S. Army's Human Terrain System (HTS) (see Forte, 2011a; González, 2009; Kelly et al., 2010; Price, 2009).

From there I invite readers to consider the extent to which anthropologists in academia are positioned as insiders and first-hand witnesses to militarism, and more broadly, imperialism. I will argue that anthropologists, as members of institutions that increasingly serve the powerful, are positioned in a way where critique matters more than ever. An anti-imperialist anthropology serves to challenge the current militarization and corporatization underway in the society as a whole.

Moving beyond these observations and arguments, the central aim then becomes one of considering what "anthropology against empire" would look like, that is, one less amenable to cooptation, one that produces the "wrong" messages for power, and chooses the "wrong" focus: respectively, a critique of the powerful and the centres of power themselves. This requires a change in how anthropologists define their "fields," as well as a transformation in our methods, and the kinds of questions we ask. To rework anthropology into something that does not serve the powerful, that does not seek "authorization," and that does not lust after recognition and rewards from the powerful, should involve "ethnography in reverse" among other methods.

Ethnography in reverse recognizes that to make the familiar strange—where that which is most familiar to us as academics is the routine and everyday corporatization of university business and the intrusion of the national security state in setting the agenda for research—we need to alienate ourselves from the norm of our own working environment. It is an alienation that can also be understood as revolt. This is "studying up" (Nader, 1969), where we recognize academic anthropology as a firm part of the "up"— maybe not the very *top* of the political-economic pyramid, but certainly *up there*. Ethnography in reverse is not just a way of making the familiar strange, but what we hope will go further as a productive form of estrangement that takes this form: what is strange becomes questionable for its arbitrariness, so what are the other intellectual and political possibilities that we can envision? If within academic anthropology we can create a way of thinking that is *against* empire, hopefully we will be in a better position to discern new forms of anthropology that could come *after* empire.

Anthropology, Militarism, Imperialism

"No one in the world today is untouched by militarism," Gusterson argues, adding: "militarism is integral to global society today" (2007, p. 156). Rather than providing a definition of militarism, he produces a spectrum of manifestations of militarism that can be taken as the foundation of a working definition. He says that militarism, "can be seen around the world in the presence of standing armies, paramilitaries, and military contractors; the stockpiling of weaponry; burgeoning state surveillance programs; the colonization of research by the national security state; the circulation of militarized imagery in popular culture...and [quoting Lutz] 'the shaping of national histories in ways that glorify and legitimate military action'" (2007, p. 156). To this we could add here the global proliferation of roughly a thousand U.S. military installations (Johnson, 2000; Lutz, 2009).

Opening up to the kind of challenge which I want to add, Gusterson notes that "war and militarism have stood in the same kind of relationship to anthropology as has colonialism" (2007, p. 156). His criticism is that anthropologists have not only written little about contemporary wars and international relations, but that they have written even less about their own relations with the national security state (Gusterson, 2007, p. 156). This is truly remarkable, as Gusterson and others have noted, given the bedrock for anthropology in the Indian Wars in the U.S., how World War I created the conditions for Malinowski's work in the Trobriand Islands, how Ruth Benedict's classic on Japanese character was a perfect example of anthropological work commissioned by the national security state, how other American anthropologists worked as administrators in Japanese internment camps, and how during the early decades of the Cold War most anthropologists learned to either not ask the wrong questions, where the state was concerned, or avoided areas engulfed in war, and yet showed strong interest for research that was oriented toward serving the national security state, such as national character studies and area studies. This was largely the imperial condition of anthropology at least until the 1960s, one that existed even if it did not encompass all anthropologists, and even if it was questioned by some of those whom it employed. While some will point to Franz Boas' certainly courageous effort to denounce anthropologists working as spies during World War I, one wonders if they can recall that this stance also earned him a lifetime censure by the American Anthropological Association, an organization he helped to found, and that the censure was only lifted in 2005, that is, after 86 years (AAA, 2005).

One side of this new challenge calls for anthropological work on militarism that at least equals what we have for capitalism, colonialism, and globalization (Gusterson, 2007, p. 165). Yet, despite anthropologists' first-hand contact with colonial situations, as ethnographers in British colonies in Africa, the Caribbean, and the Pacific for most of the twentieth century, it was not until 1972, well after a wave of formal decolonization had begun, that we saw the first article actually about colonialism in an anthropology journal, and even then it was not authored by an anthropologist (Horvath, 1972). If we were to be more generous, the argument could be made to extend the timeline back a couple of years (for example, Helms, 1969, and Patterson, 1971). Otherwise, for the most part, anthropologists largely pushed into the background the colonization processes that reshaped "the field" in which they studied, magnifying the tribe and blurring the empire. This is a point that has abundantly been made already by anthropologists such as

Eric Wolf and Jonathan Friedman. The point of this is that we should not be satisfied, as if we had a robust corpus of work on colonialism, or even contemporary imperialism, in anthropology. I believe that studies of militarism make most sense in the context in which the most acute militarism actually occurs: in aggressive imperial centres, and to a lesser extent in some parts of the periphery that seek to actively resist and defend themselves against imperial aggression.

The first point I would make here is that I do not advocate making the study of militarism into an autonomous field of inquiry, when speaking of our own militarization makes most sense in the context of a broader framework of imperialist interventions. Gusterson himself says that what we need is "a set of texts that analyze militarism in relation to nationalism, late modern capitalism, media cultures, and the state while mapping the ways in which militarism remakes communities, public cultures, and the consciousness of individual subjects in multiple geographic and social locations" (2007, p. 165). A second point is that the study of militarism, even if narrowly construed, is a study that transcends disciplinary boundaries, just as anthropologists studying capitalism, nationalism, etc., have done so in dialogue with a wider body of work in multiple disciplines. The third point is that is that we need a better understanding of the instrument that is seeking to produce this knowledge about militarism. This would then be a project that also focuses on how institutionalized and professionalized anthropology is itself one of those entities that fits in with capitalism, the state, and the national security establishment, either very directly, or in reaction against it. Such a project would also consider how new compromises and new silences accommodate the domestic penetration of the national security state at home, and the rise to dominance of a "humanitarian" imperialist mission for countries such as Canada.

Anthropology ought to be inherently anti-war and anti-empire, if academic anthropologists took seriously their own commitment to mutual understanding, respect for difference, and peaceful coexistence and interaction among diverse cultures. Unfortunately, we must remember what David Price, another prominent researcher and critic of anthropology's ties to the national security state, has to say about anthropology: "while many anthropologists express concerns about disciplinary ties to military and intelligence organizations, contemporary anthropology has no core with which to either sync or collide and there are others in the field who openly (and quietly) support such developments" (Price, 2005a). Nor can the critique of imperialism emerge primarily or solely from ethnography as such.

An anthropology of militarism ought to start at home first, the location with which we are most familiar, and it could begin by focusing on the university which serves as the institutional and intellectual context of our research efforts. We should first begin by understanding the militarization of anthropology since it offers us an intimate angle on the pervasive spread of militarism, and of the ethos of counterinsurgency and pacification. Anthropologists are themselves the actors in the setting which they aim to understand. Inspired by John Murra, Frank Salomon argues that "instead of claiming innocence by virtue of Third World solidarity, or of objectivity, or of theoretical transcendence, anthropologists should recognize themselves as players put haphazardly into a world of dangerous power and do something good with that situation" (2007, p. 794). Rather than only hold a mirror up to powerless others, anthropologists should translate our discipline's state of being for a wider audience, especially those traditionally researched in the discipline, to explain how we have been, and still can be, used as the eyes, ears, advisers, and policy planners of the imperial state. Doing something good with our situation, as Salomon puts it, might mean better equipping marginalized and subordinated communities and persons to understand the operations of the state and the knowledge-production industries in seeking to keep them under surveillance and to control their lives—this would be true collaboration. This takes ethical research beyond that which is minimally constrained to mere research procedures, such as informed consent for interviews.

Anthropology as the Terrain of the Military and Intelligence Apparatuses

The U.S. Department of Defense may in fact be the single largest employer of anthropologists anywhere in the world, employing 532 persons with anthropology degrees, including 58 with a PhD (Forte, 2011b). Beyond anthropology alone, as far back as 1988 a CIA spokesperson boasted that the CIA had enough professors under contract "to staff a large university" (Mills, 1991, p. 37). Prior to that, former CIA Personnel Director F.W.M. Janney wrote: "It is absolutely essential that the Agency have available to it the greatest single source of expertise: the American academic community" (Zwerling, 2011, p. 27). David Price (2005a, 2005b, 2008) and others have identified several intelligence programs that fund the university education of young students, with the contractual obligation that they serve the CIA, or other intelligence units (there are in excess of 1,000 of them—see Priest & Arkin, 2010), but without disclosing their intelligence ties to either other students or professors who may also be the target of their spying. And beyond formal programs, General David Petraeus encourages all academics to act as the eyes and ears of the Pentagon when traveling abroad (Mazzetti, 2010). (A great example of recruiting academics in general to serve as the eyes and ears of the state is the newly formed "Cultural Knowledge Consortium" at culturalknowledge.org—see also the discussion in Price [2012].) If anything, the militarization and securitization of academia in North America (and parts of western Europe) has not only been resurgent, it has been also been proliferating more programs with more funding, especially since "9/11".

In terms of intelligence programs on U.S. campuses (in Canada we may be importing some of their graduates when we hire from the U.S.), these include: the Pat Roberts Intelligence Scholars Program (PRISP), formed with the guidance and active support of an anthropology professor, Felix Moos, at the University of Kansas; the National Security Education Program (NSEP); the Intelligence Community Scholars Program (ICSP); the National Academic Consortium for Homeland Security (NACHOS); and, an array of private think tanks that link social science research to the so-called "global war on terror" with some of these, like the Hoover Institution at Stanford, housed on campuses. One could also include the presence of the Reserve Officers' Training Corps (ROTC) on many U.S. campuses.

Among the new initiatives that link U.S. campuses to the national security state is the National Consortium for the Study of Terrorism and Responses to Terrorism (START) which came into being with the passage of the Homeland Security Act in 2002 (Public Law 107-296, 2002). Section 308 of that act announced the intent to establish a "coordinated, university-based system to enhance the nation's homeland security". Several "centers of excellence" were established in U.S. universities, with the leading one being the University of Maryland's, whose purpose is summarized as informing "decisions on how to disrupt terrorists and terrorist groups through empirically-grounded findings on the human element of the terrorist threat" (Department of Homeland Security [DHS], 2012). Research at Maryland's START (2010) is divided into three working groups. One looks at "terrorist group formation and recruitment". The primary concern of this working group is "radicalization". The second working group focuses on "terrorist group persistence". In describing the "pyramid of terrorism," included at its base by START are "all who sympathize with terrorist goals, even though they may disagree with terrorists' attacks on civilians". If anti-imperialism were cited as a "terrorist goal" it would mean that many critical academics would be considered as being at the base of this terrorist pyramid. The third working group has to do with "societal responses to terrorist threats and attacks," an inclusive program that seeks to bring its findings down to the level of "household and community preparedness for terrorist attacks". Anthropologists are among the 65 researchers working in the START program, which derives its senior advisors from the military, intelligence, and defence contracting industry.

The U.S. Department of Defense also directly funds academic research oriented toward "counter-terrorism," commencing in 2008 with its "Minerva Initiative" (2012). The Pentagon is especially interested in identifying undefined "terrorist" networks, ideologies, and communities amenable to hosting terrorists are concerned, and how to counter them (DoD, 2008, p. 20; Center for the Study of Religion and Conflict [CSRC], 2012). Minerva is also open to funding Canadian researchers (DoD, 2008, p. 4), funding one at the University of Guelph for a project on the manipulation of group threats (see IU, 2009). Minerva also funds the work of at least one anthropologist (CSRC, 2012). Compared to Canada's Social Sciences and Humanities Research Council (SSHRC) grants, which until recently offered a $250,000 maximum to cover a three-year period, or a Canada Research Chair, which can a little over $1 million for five years, Minerva can pay up to $3 million for one year (DoD, 2008, p. 4), and one recipient has won a $10 million grant to cover three years (Forte, 2009a, 2009b).

Among the Minerva Initiative's goals, of direct concern to anthropologists, is "the development of models and approaches to study behavior networks, groups, and communities over time," in effect a program of academic-directed surveillance—here anthropologists are specifically called upon, as "the relevance of context and situation may require field research" (DoD, 2008, p. 20). The Pentagon further adds that "there is an urgent need to be able to locate the points of influence and characterize the processes necessary to influence populations that harbor terrorist organizations in diverse cultures as well as individuals who identify with terrorist group figures" (DoD, 2008, p. 20). This clearly points to academics playing a role in extending the intelligence-gathering capacities of the national security state. Making this even more explicit, the Pentagon explained that what would be "especially helpful" to it is,

> "understanding where organized violence is likely to erupt, what factors might explain its contagion, and how to circumvent its spread. Research on belief formation and emotional contagion will provide cultural advisors with better tools to understand the impact of operations on the local population. This research should also contribute to countermeasures to help revise or influence belief structures to reduce the likelihood of militant cells forming". (DoD, 2008, p. 21)

The Minerva Initiative is not simply "imposed" on academia, as much as it is a program conceived by the government and not by universities. Academic institutions also play a role in legitimating Minerva. For example, in 2008 the National Science Foundation (NSF), with the support of the American Anthropological Association (AAA), successfully lobbied to administer $8 million of the Pentagon's $75 million for Minerva, offering their collective seal of approval to projects by offering their own, semi-independent peer review (Glenn, 2008; NSF, 2008a). Indeed, the main argument produced by the AAA's then president, Setha Low (2008), was simply that anthropologists and other academics ought to be the ones offering peer review for the program—and thus leaving unchallenged the degree to which Minerva incorporates academics into an effort that encourages the application of ethnographic fieldwork in labeling local networks as "terrorist," identifying their leaders, and proposing ways to defeat them. The NSF for its part boasted of its long service to the national security state: "To secure the national defense was one of the original missions we were given when we were chartered in 1950," said David Lightfoot, assistant director of NSF's Social, Behavioral and Economic Sciences Directorate, "we've always believed that sociologists, anthropologists, psychologists and other social scientists, through basic social and behavioral science research, could benefit our national security. In fact, we've always done so through various research projects" (NSF, 2008b). Craig Calhoun, president of the Social Science Research Council, at a 2008 Minerva workshop organized and hosted by the Pentagon, went on the record cheerfully praising Minerva and calling for more ways of expanding the nature and range of academic collaboration with the military and intelligence communities (Calhoun, 2008).

Another joint effort between the Pentagon and academia comes in the form of the alliance between Florida International University and U.S. Southern Command (SOUTHCOM) (see Pine, 2010). In this case Latin Americanists are drafting research papers around the concept of "strategic culture," which is a way of reframing domestic social relations, politics, and history, in strategic terms. As Adrienne Pine explained, "by reframing corporate-military strategy as 'culture', FIU-SOUTHCOM intentionally draws upon the legitimacy and integrity of anthropology and other social sciences to depoliticize and bolster its case for military occupation of the Americas" (Pine, 2010).

What is common to both START and Minerva is a series of assumptions of causation that are meant to direct academic researchers away from thinking about systemic questions of imperialism, military intervention, or even just U.S. foreign policy in narrow terms. In other words, the problem with the Other, *is the Other*—hardly a construction that would satisfy most anthropologists, but that is how they are effectively asked to "adjust" themselves in their thinking when they join these efforts. These programs assume an innocent and benign U.S., which does not suffer "blowback" from its actions abroad but is instead the victim of "radicalization," itself rooted in religious contagion (hence emotion and irrationality). This is similar to the assumption that grounds the U.S. Army's Human Terrain System (more below): conflict is rooted in "cultural misunderstanding," and *resistance to invasion and occupation* is thus automatically dispelled, in advance. (This reminds me of a common theme found in motivational speakers' prescriptions for "self-improvement": the real problem in your life is *your attitude*.)

Not all of the programs that weld anthropology to the national security state are top-down creations: some emerge from the efforts of anthropologists themselves. "I've been with would-be martyrs and holy warriors from Morocco's Atlantic shore to Indonesia's outer islands, and from Gaza to Kashmir," as anthropologist Scott Atran boasted to the U.S. Senate Armed Services Subcommittee on Emerging Threats and Capabilities (Atran, 2010, p. 2), in his capacity as director of research for ARTIS Research and Risk Modeling (ARTIS, 2012). In marketing his services to the Subcommittee, noting that there was inadequate funding from the state, Atran declared:

> "If you want to be successful in the long run where it counts—in stopping the next and future generations of disaffected youth from finding their life's meaning in the thrill and adventure of joining their friends in taking on the world's mightiest power...then you have to understand these pathways that take young people to and from political and group violence. Then, knowing these pathways, you can do what needs to be done". (2010, p. 2)

Atran is explicitly against embedding social scientists in military units in combat zones. What is his project is about, however, is providing research on areas of particular concern to the U.S. and in particular, "Preventing radicalization...Countering radicalization...De-radicalizing those who have committed to violence" (Atran, 2010, p. 6).

In the U.S. the major recent effort to militarize anthropology, one that is ongoing, and that reportedly may be replicated by the Canadian Defence Forces (AJP, 2010a; Bertuca, 2010), is the U.S. Army's Human Terrain System (see Forte, 2011a), which embeds academics in counterinsurgency units to gather cultural intelligence, map social networks, assist in psychological operations, and try to "win hearts and minds". HTS has recently identified universities as the best training grounds for their candidates (Forte, 2011b), rather than the military's own in-house training, a fact that potentially turns many academics, even those opposed to HTS, into unknowing potential trainers for the program. Should plans to reproduce this in Canada actually materialize, and should the Canadian Forces seek to recruit academics, one imagine the possibilities with over 400 PhD students currently in anthropology (Forte, 2010a), and an academic job market that might only absorb the tiniest fraction of them, and even then mostly as part-time instructors. In the U.S., the salary for a HTS employee exceeds $200,000 per year when deployed (Forte, 2011a, p. 150).

HTS is by no means the only vehicle for supplying the military with research by anthropologists. There are several other institutional means by which academics can, as in General Petraeus' formulation (Mazzetti, 2010), engage in "intelligence gathering...to identify militants and provide 'persistent situational awareness,' while forging ties to local indigenous groups". One clear case involved the Bowman Expeditions of the American Geographic Society, as part of its México Indígena project, denounced as geopiracy by the organization of Zapotecas , the *Unión de Organizaciones de la Sierra Juárez* (UNOSJO). The AGS' project took place in Oaxaca and San Luis Potosí, México from 2005, and was financed by the Foreign Military Studies Office (FMSO) of the U.S. Department of Defense and involved a private military contractor, Radiance Technologies (Forte, 2010b). Native communities were unaware of who funded the project, or how the information that was elicited would be used. Moreover, they did not consent to having their personal information, maps of their lands, and traditional knowledge uploaded to a military database, the same one to which HTS uploads its data—the World Basic Information Library (WBIL). The Zapotecas denounced the AGS for extracting information for the purposes of a broader form of globalized counterinsurgency as witnessed by Mexico and which "consists of the privatization of communal lands as part of a strategy of neoliberalism and counterinsurgency" (Forte, 2010b). Here too Canadian academics have participated—specifically, Carleton University (AJP, 2011).

Academic Militarization in Canada

The militarization of academia in Canada is not too far behind the U.S., even if we do not yet see the same degree of incorporation of anthropology into the national security establishment. Most large Canadian universities receive research funding from the Department of National Defence, and in particular the Security Defence Forum (see Beach, 2011) channels military funding to 14 universities and their centers of expertise in the social sciences. Funding also comes in the form of "corporate research partnerships and donation agreements which are not held to the same requirements of transparency as federal funds" with corporations sometimes subcontracting universities to complete work commissioned by them from the federal government (Beach, 2011). At my own university, Concordia, five of the CEOs who recently led the Board of Governors had direct links to the military-industrial complex, and the university is a participant in Project Hero (see Beach, 2011). The university has also marked as one of its "signature areas" the "Will to Intervene" project that advocates direct and immediate military intervention in cases such as Libya, for example. In parts of the campus, the university showcases its aerial drones. At least one of our American-trained professors in political science conducts research related to counterinsurgency, with funding from the DND for work on Afghanistan and Pakistan.

In addition, I also documented a case of militarized anthropology at the University of Calgary, with a formal position in military anthropology sponsored by the Canadian Defence and Foreign Affairs Institute. The University of Calgary's Department of Anthropology openly refused to answer any of the basic questions that were posed, seeking information that any applicant and referee would need to know, and specifically addressing issues of academic freedom, ethics, and the intended applications of the research (AJP, 2010b).

At the very least, both the infrastructure and some early experiments are already in place for militarizing Canadian anthropology. With more interventionist governments sending Canadian forces into conflicts around the world, and with heightened military spending, we should be very alert as to what may be coming, especially as the desire for "humanitarian intervention," has crossed all party lines in the Canadian federal parliament.

Anthropology for Empire

Where the employment of anthropologists in support of the national security state is concerned, this is a repeat, or perhaps a continuation, of the long history of anthropological service to expansionist states, colonial management, and imperial domination, a history with which institutional anthropology has yet to come to terms. The minimal number of courses, anywhere, dedicated to decolonizing anthropology, as well as the relative paucity of literature in this area, attests to a kind of a collective allergic reaction to self-critique which, if anything, has become entrenched as part of a decades-long reactionary backlash against the arguably light and partial critiques represented by the *Writing Culture* phenomenon (see Argyrou, 2002). This is not say that anthropology does not contain within it a significant critical and even activist tradition, especially since the 1960s, as much as it is to suggest that anthropology has no real core, as David Price argued, with which to either align or collide with state power.

Among anthropologists there can be several motivations for aligning their work with the interests of the imperial state, and this can be witnessed from times that pre-date anthropology's institutional birth to the present. Among these motivations, some of which we can rank as convention, we can include: the persistent,

perceived need to promote the relevance and usefulness of anthropology, and thus seizing on the interest of the military and intelligence communities as an avenue for becoming "relevant"; the
ingrained practice of bemoaning the lack of attention from other
disciplines and the wider society; the drive to develop applied anthropology, and to provide training for gainful employment; in the
U.S. especially, disciplinary self-promotion as a "science" that
should be valued, recognized, and rewarded by those in power; for
some, the goal of helping to "do good"; and, the basic foundation of
the discipline, which literally involves selling knowledge of the
other—the debate here (when there is any) being one that is about
the appropriate clientele.

What is often underestimated, or understated, or simply mis-
understood by those who argue that the impact of military-funded
research is either negligible or neutral, is the degree to which we
gradually adjust university structures to increased militarization
and toward producing research that either fits in with militarist
objectives, or does not challenge them. This point of view was best
expressed by Gusterson (2008):

> "When research that could be funded by neutral civilian
> agencies is instead funded by the military, knowledge is subtly
> militarized and bent in the way a tree is bent by a prevailing
> wind. The public comes to accept that basic academic research
> on religion and violence 'belongs' to the military; scholars who
> never saw themselves as doing military research now do;
> maybe they wonder if their access to future funding is best
> secured by not criticizing U.S. foreign policy; a discipline
> whose independence from military and corporate funding
> fueled the kind of critical thinking a democracy needs is now
> compromised; and the priorities of the military further define
> the basic terms of public and academic debate".

Price (2008) made a similar argument concerning the problems
of conforming research "with the ideological positions of a powerful
state". The really provocative question, therefore, is about how
much American anthropological research—influential as it is in
Canada and elsewhere—has already been long subject to such
pressures to conform. Indeed, this also means that anthropologists, at least in the U.S., have long been positioned as *insiders* in
the processes of militarization and securitization, and now we
should capitalize on that knowledge by exposing it and explaining
it. The challenge, taken on by Price, is that,

"In...anthropology, there is an overwhelming disciplinary amnesia of the extent to which research has been directed by the Pentagon and intelligence agencies in the past....there has been a broad spectrum of overt and covert control over this funding control, with the full range running from the rampant secret directing of funding of unwitting scholars doing research of interest to the CIA and others, to the open, massive funding of a full spectrum of social science and language projects through agencies like the NSF or Fulbright Programs". (Price, 2008)

However, it is not just of matter of what kind of institution gets to fund research, but also the nature of the research itself, the questions it asks, the answers it seeks, and the intended outcomes of the research. In other words, it is quite possible for research to be militarized without any funding at all from any military source, that is, research that could be useful for purposes of surveillance and counterinsurgency.

Anthropology against Empire

If the infrastructure, financing, and the rationale are all in place, we need to also consider how the very structure and mode of doing anthropology are themselves amenable to militarization. Our obsessive focus on ethnography of subordinate groups, as if anthropology were locating in a method/tradition its much sought after influence and recognition of its contribution, opens up a major vulnerability. By insisting on a mode of knowledge production that has us probing and inserting ourselves among those without the same institutional firewalls and prohibited access we find among states and corporate elites, the kinds of institutional blocks that impede conventional ethnographic fieldwork, we ensure that we continue to mine the lives and minds of the ruled, the oppressed, and the subordinated. In particular, we often run the risk of making marginalized groups legible to the authorities, under the guise of speaking truth to power (see Forte, 2010c; 2007; 2008). What about translating power for the powerless? Telling the truth about the powerful, as we ourselves are members of institutions that are assemblages of political and economic power, that serve power, logically presents itself as one of our special areas of knowledge, one so routine and everyday that it seems many of us take it for granted, and turn our heads to look elsewhere, often very far away, for the supposed truths of power.

Our own colonial predispositions need to be unveiled, starting from relatively small matters of enduring terminology where we refer to societies and peoples as "the field," and the so-called problem of "going native" (using a phrase, and raising an alarm, that is to be found among intelligence agencies and diplomatic missions), to the impulse among some students to get professional certification in anthropology so that they can get jobs in NGOs and "help people"—often far away people conveniently imagined as desperate, with gaunt faces and outstretched hands, begging for us to solve their problems, without pausing to think how work at home might help to stop our society and its leadership from creating problems for these overseas others to start with. Instead, anthropology, interventionist and humanitarian, becomes part of a global SPCA, part of the zoology of imperialism, as we market our special insights on animal management. A discipline that often seems bent on arbitrating, regulating, and monitoring indigenous identities and practices, may be called anthropology, or it may be called by its more obvious name: counterinsurgency. Our job is to build on and advance that part of anthropology that is not aligned to power, and that takes domination as its central concern.

Rather than producing more research that exposes marginalized communities to the readings of the powerful, and going further by making such research more easily accessible ("open access"), I am advocating different paths out of empire. First, our broader effort would involve reexamining institutional anthropology as a particular mode of knowledge production that is indicative of a Western way of consuming and possibly even managing non-Western others. This also involves a critical reexamination of why we do anthropology, what is anthropology, and what is the purpose of such knowledge, and whether it should be pursued as a discipline. Second, rather than only train our students to observe basic principles of ethical conduct in research, we should start dialogues with those traditionally targeted as objects of ethnography to develop knowledge about what they can do to better protect themselves from unscrupulous research projects. Third, when working with persons and communities that do not occupy a high point in the political and economic power structure, we might consider collaborating in new ways—not collaborating to produce more about the powerless, which is semi-collaboration at best, but a genuine collaboration that involves a partnership in unmasking the workings of power, sharing our results with the wider public, and mutually reexamining the situation of the anthropologist and his/her partners in light of that research. Fourth, since "non-Western others" are increasingly speaking directly, and for themselves, to the wider world, we might consider "open source ethnography" which deals with local documentary creations that are intended for a public audience, therefore not secret or inaccessible knowledge, and where we engage in a form of commentary as ethnography (see Fabian, 2008). Fifth, what I term "WikiLeakism"—research using leaked state documents—can also give rise to a series of ethnographic encounters that allows us access in unusual ways to centres of power that are normally closed to us (for more, see González, 2012). These are some of the primary ways I have sought to take anthropology out of the imperial domain, working for an anthropology that is against empire, and that has a chance of existing in some form after empire.

References

American Anthropological Association (AAA). (2005). Uncensoring Franz Boas. American Anthropological Association. http://aaanet.org/about/Policies/Uncensoring-Franz-Boas.cfm

Anthropologists for Justice and Peace (AJP). (2010a). A Resurgent Human Terrain System: Concerns for Anthropology, Including Canada. *Anthropologists for Justice and Peace*, December 13. http://anthrojustpeace.blogspot.com/2010/12/resurgent-human-terrain-system-concerns.html

————. (2010b). Militarizing Anthropology at the University of Calgary. *Anthropologists for Justice and Peace*, December 13. http://anthrojustpeace.blogspot.com/2010/12/militarizing-anthropology-at-university.html

————. (2011). Anthropology, the Military, Global and Domestic Counterinsurgency. *Anthropologists for Justice and Peace*, June 12. http://anthrojustpeace.blogspot.com/2011/06/anthropology-military-global-and.html

Argyrou, V. (2002). *Anthropology and the Will to Meaning: A Postcolonial Critique*. London: Pluto Press.

ARTIS. (2012). http://artisresearch.com/

Atran, S. (2010). Pathways to and From Violent Extremism: The Case for Science-Based Field Research. Statement before the Senate Armed Services Subcommittee on Emerging Threats & Capabilities. http://artisresearch.com/articles/ARTIS%20-%20Atran%20-%20Testimony%20-%20Senate%20Armed%20Services%2010%20March%202010.pdf

Beach, L. (2011). Canadian Academic Institutions, the Weapons Industry, and Militarist Ideology. In Maximilian C. Forte (ed.), *The*

New Imperialism, Vol. II: Interventionism, Information Warfare, and the Military-Academic Complex (pp. 15–43). Montreal: Alert Press.

Bertuca, T. (2010). Army Increasing Number of Human Terrain Teams; Advising Allies. *InsideDefense.com Newsstand.*
http://defensenewsstand.com/NewsStand-General/The-INSIDER-Free-Article/army-increasing-number-of-human-terrain-teams-advising-allies/menu-id-720.html

Calhoun, C. (2008). Minerva Research Initiative.
http://youtube.com/watch?feature=player_embedded&v=VuSOvmWPg60

Center for the Study of Religion and Conflict (CSRC). (2012). Finding Allies: Mapping Counter-Radical Muslim Discourse.
http://csrc.asu.edu/research/projects/mapping-counterradical-discourse

Department of Defense, U.S. (DoD). (2008). Broad Agency Announcement. BAA Announcement Number No. WF911NF-08-R-0007. Washington D.C.: U.S. Department of Defense.
http://box.net/shared/o9ibfu2n3f

Department of Homeland Security, U.S. (DHS). (2012). Homeland Security Centers of Excellence.
http://dhs.gov/files/programs/editorial_0498.shtm

Fabian, J. (2008). *Ethnography as Commentary: Writing from the Virtual Archive.* Durham NC: Duke University Press.

Forte, M. C. (2007). Exposing the Network. *Zero Anthropology*, December 28.
http://zeroanthropology.net/2007/12/28/exposing-the-network/

———— . (2008). Imperializing Open Access and Militarizing Open Source: 'What's yours is ours. What's ours is ours'. *Zero Anthropology.*, August 18.
http://zeroanthropology.net/2008/08/18/imperializing-open-access-and-militarizing-open-source-whats-yours-is-ours-whats-ours-is-ours/

———— . (2009a). What are the Pentagon's Minerva Researchers Doing? *Zero Anthropology*, June 12.
http://zeroanthropology.net/2009/06/12/what-are-the-pentagons-minerva-researchers-doing/

———— . (2009b). News from the Military-Academic Complex: McFate's PhD, HTS Contracts, Minerva Grants, Afghanistan. *Zero Anthropology*, October 14.
http://zeroanthropology.net/2009/10/14/news-from-the-military-academic-complex-mcfates-phd-hts-contracts-minerva-grants-afghanistan/

———— . (2010a). Anthropology in Canada: Number of Students, Female Percentage. *Zero Anthropology*, October 5.
http://zeroanthropology.net/2010/10/05/anthropology-in-canada-number-of-students-female-percentage/

———— . (2010b). Human Terrain System Video News: John Stanton,

and the AGS Bowman Expeditions in Mexico. *Zero Anthropology*, June 3.
http://zeroanthropology.net/2010/06/03/human-terrain-system-video-news-john-stanton-and-the-ags-bowman-expeditions-in-mexico/

———. (2010c). Ethnographies of Resistance Movements: Legible to the Authorities". *Zero Anthropology*, October 11.
http://zeroanthropology.net/2010/10/11/ethnographies-of-resistance-movements-legibile-to-the-authorities/

———. (2011a). The Human Terrain System and Anthropology: A Review of Ongoing Public Debates. *American Anthropologist*, 113(1), 149–153.

———. (2011b). Declaring the U.S. Army's Human Terrain System a Success: Rereading the CNA Report. *Zero Anthropology*, February 19.
http://zeroanthropology.net/2011/02/19/declaring-the-u-s-army%E2%80%99s-human-terrain-system-a-success-rereading-the-cna-report/

Fulbright, J. W. (1967). A Point of View. *Science*, December 22, 1555.

Glenn, D. (2008). NSF Invites Proposals for Pentagon-Sponsored Research Program. *The Chronicle of Higher Education*, August 1.
http://chronicle.com/article/NSF-Invites-Proposals-for/1033

González, R. J. (2009). *American Counterinsurgency: Human Science and the Human Terrain*. Chicago IL: Prickly Paradigm Press.

———. (2012). Anthropology and the Covert: Methodological Notes on Researching Military and Intelligence Programs. *Anthropology Today*, 28(2), April, 21–25.

Gregory, D. (2008). The Rush to the Intimate: Counterinsurgency and the Cultural Turn. *Radical Philosophy*, 150 (July–August).
http://radicalphilosophy.com/default.asp?channel_id=2369&editorial_id=26755

Gusterson, H. (2007). Anthropology and Militarism. *Annual Review of Anthropology*, 36, 155–75.

———. (2008). The U.S. Military's Quest to Weaponize Culture. *Bulletin of the Atomic Scientists*, June 20.
http://thebulletin.org/web-edition/columnists/hugh-gusterson/the-us-militarys-quest-to-weaponize-culture

Helms, M. W. (1969). The Cultural Ecology of a Colonial Tribe. *Ethnology*, 8, 1, January, 76–84.

Horvath, R. J. (1972). A Definition of Colonialism. *Current Anthropology*, 13, 1, February, 45–57.

IU. (2009). IU sociologist receives NSF award to study how groups behave under threat. *IU News Room*, May 3.
http://newsinfo.iu.edu/news/page/normal/12352.html

Johnson, C. (2000). *Blowback: The Costs and Consequences of American Empire*. New York: Henry Holt and Company.

Kelly, J. D.; Jauregui, B.; Mitchell, S. T.; & Walton, J. (eds.). (2010). *Anthropology and Global Counterinsurgency*. Chicago IL: University of Chicago Press.

Low, S. (2008). Letter to the Honorable Jim Nussle, the Office of Management and Budget. *American Anthropological Association*, May 28.

http://aaanet.org/issues/policy-advocacy/upload/minerva-letter.pdf

Lutz, C. (2009). Anthropology in an Era of Permanent War. *Anthropologica*, 51, 2, 367–379.

Mazzetti, M. (2010). U.S. Is Said to Expand Secret Actions in Mideast. *The New York Times*, May 24.

Mills, A. C. (1991). *C.I.A. Off Campus: Building the Movement against Agency Recruitment and Research*. Boston MA: South End Press.

Minerva Intiative. (2012). The Minerva Initiative.

http://minerva.dtic.mil/

Nader, L. (1969). Up the Anthropologist: Perspectives Gained from Studying Up. In Dell Hymes (ed.) *Reinventing Anthropology*, (pp. 284–311). New York: Vintage Books.

National Science Foundation (NSF). (2008a). Social and Behavioral Dimensions of National Security, Conflict, and Cooperation (NSCC).

http://nsf.gov/funding/pgm_summ.jsp?pims_id=503294&org=NSF&sel_org=NSF&from=fund

————— . (2008b). NSF Issues Solicitation for Basic, Human Sciences Research on Social and Behavioral Dimensions of National Security, Conflict and Cooperation. Press Release 08-133.

http://nsf.gov/news/news_summ.jsp?cntn_id=112015

Patterson, P. (1971). The Colonial Parallel: A View of Indian History. *Ethnohistory*, 18(1), 1–17.

Pine, A. (2010). An Urgent Message to Academics about SOUTHCOM. *Quotha*, November 4.

http://quotha.net/node/1302

Price, D. H. (2005a). The CIA's Campus Spies: Exposing the Pat Roberts Intelligence Scholars Program. *CounterPunch*, March 12–13.

http://counterpunch.org/price03122005.html

————— . (2005b). Carry on Spying (or Pay Us Back at the Rate of 2,400 Per Cent): CIA Skullduggery in Academia. *CounterPunch*, May 22.

http://counterpunch.org/2005/05/21/carry-on-spying-or-pay-us-back-at-the-rate-of-2-400-per-cent/

————— . (2008). Social Science in Harness: Inside the Minerva Consortium. *CounterPunch*, June 24.

http://counterpunch.org/2008/06/24/social-science-in-harness/

————— . (2009). Counterinsurgency, Anthropology and Disciplinary Complicity: Roberto González on Human Terrain Systems. *CounterPunch*, February 3.

http://counterpunch.org/2009/02/03/counterinsurgency-anthropology-and-disciplinary-complicity/

————— . (2012). Counterinsurgency and the M-VICO System: Human

Relations Area Files and Anthropology's Dual-Use Legacy. *Anthropology Today*, 28(1), 16–20.

Priest, D., & Arkin, W. M. (2010). A Hidden World, Growing beyond Control. *The Washington Post*, July 19.

Public Law 107-296. (2002). An Act to establish the Department of Homeland Security, and for other purposes. 107th Congress, November 25.

http://dhs.gov/xlibrary/assets/hr_5005_enr.pdf

Renzi, F. (2006). Networds: Terra Incognita and the Case for Ethnographic Intelligence. *Military Review*, September–October.

http://usacac.leavenworth.army.mil/CAC/milreview/English/sepoct06/Renzi.pdf

Salomon, F. (2007). John Victor Murra (1916–2006). *American Anthropologist*, 109(4), December, 792–796.

START. (2010). National Consortium for the Study of Terrorism and Responses to Terrorism: A Center of Excellence of the U.S. Department of Homeland Security based at the University of Maryland.

http://start.umd.edu/start/

Zwerling, P. (2011). Template for Terror. In Philip Zwerling (ed.), *The CIA On Campus: Essays on Academic Freedom and the National Security State*, (pp. 7–32). Jefferson NC: McFarland & Company Inc., Publishers.

CONTRIBUTORS

Philip Capozzi is from Montreal, Quebec, and has recently completed his BA Major in Anthropology and Minor in Sociology at Concordia University in Montreal. His focal research interests are environmental studies, community development, and studies in food sovereignty and security. He has since applied to an MSc in Marketing at the University of HEC in Montreal, Quebec.

Maximilian C. Forte is the director of the New Imperialism seminar in the Department of Sociology and Anthropology, at Concordia University in Montreal, Quebec, Canada. He is also the volume editor and publisher of the New Imperialism series for Alert Press. He is an associate professor in anthropology, teaching courses in Political Anthropology, Globalization and Transnationalism, Indigenous Resurgence, Decolonizing Anthropology, and the Caribbean. His most recent book is *Slouching Towards Sirte: NATO's War on Libya and Africa* (Baraka Books).

Élie Jalbert is an anthropology student completing his BA Honours at Concordia University in Montreal at the time of publication. His current study interests include the dialectical relationship between culture and human cognintion, and the contextual susceptibility of knowledge production.

Kyle McLoughlin is finishing his BA Honours in Anthropology at Concordia University in Montreal, Quebec. His research interests and experiences are rooted in security, communities of resistance, and anti-capitalism. He hopes to continue develop his work towards a more critical and socially just anthropology.

Nathaniel Millington is from Montreal, Quebec, and obtained his D.E.C. in Criminology at Champlain College, St. Lambert, and is currently finishing his BA Specialization in Sociology and Anthropology at Concordia University in. His research focuses on the epistemology of anthropology and the relationship between overpopulation and violence.

Angela Noel is from Vancouver, British Columbia, and is undergoing her BA Joint Specialization in Sociology and Anthropology at Concordia University in Montreal, Quebec. Her primary interests are colonization, gender studies and Indigenous resurgence. She hopes to pursue a career in social work and continue studying social justice.

Nicole Pas is a sociology and anthropology specialization student, minoring in sexuality studies. She recently completed her fourth year of the BA program at Concordia university and will be returning for a final semester before pursuing post graduate studies. She hails from London, Ontario where she completed the first two years of her undergraduate degree at Western University. Her academic interests lie in identities and borders and how power and oppression flow through these essentially imagined spaces. Nicole plans to pursue a graduate degree focusing on the dynamics of race and gender—specifically focusing on how race and gender relate to the development and definition of both national and physical bodies and vice versa.

Gretchen Smith is from the Rideau Lakes, Ontario, and is working towards completing her BA in Sociology at Concordia University in Montreal, Quebec. Her focal interests lie in Indigenous studies along with political sociology. Gretchen hopes to continue her education in the sociological field.

Julian P. Stasky is a native of Westfield, Massachusetts and in his final year of BA Sociology at Concordia University in Montreal, Quebec. His primary research interests include political sociology with a focus on the effects of global economic policy and food security, especially on a community level. At the time of publication he is preparing for application to MA Sociology programs in Canada.

H. Jordane Struck is currently undertaking an MA in Socio-Cultural Anthropology at Concordia University in Montreal, Quebec. His fields of interest include the anthropology of sport, embodied experience, theories of identity, Marxism, environmentalism and theories of knowledge/power.

INDEX

www.ingramcontent.com/pod-product-compliance
Lightning Source LLC
Chambersburg PA
CBHW021340290326
41933CB00037B/283